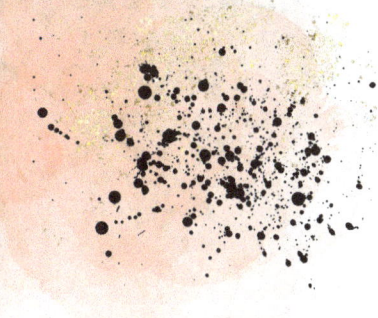

AURA COLORING ART

REVERSE
COLORING BOOK
WITH 50 INSPIRATIONAL QUOTES

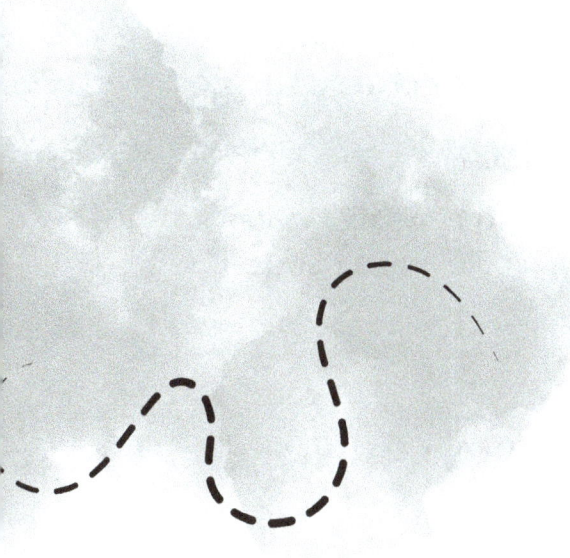
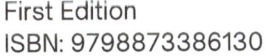
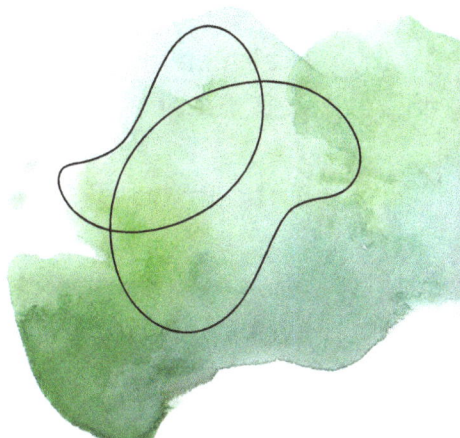

First Edition
ISBN: 9798873386130

Writer's Writing Buddy by Braulio Cabrera
Published by Aura Editions
www.auraeditions.com
© 2023 Aura Editions

All rights reserved.
This art is authorized for private use only.
No part of this book may be reproduced in any form without the permission of the publisher, except as permitted by U.S. copyright law.
To obtain permissions, contact: contact@auraeditions.com

Cover by Yosahandi Betancourt.
Illustrations © 2023 Yosahandi Betancourt.
Edited by Braulio Cabrera.

Disclaimer
The information in this book is for general informational purposes only and is not intended as professional advice. The author and publisher make no representations or warranties regarding the accuracy or completeness of the information provided and will not be held liable for any errors or omissions. The strategies and tactics discussed in this book may not be suitable for every individual or brand and readers should seek professional advice before implementing them. The author and publisher are not responsible for any negative effects that may occur as a result of using the information provided in this book.
Some links in this book are affiliate links, and if you purchase through those links, we may earn a commission at no extra cost to you.

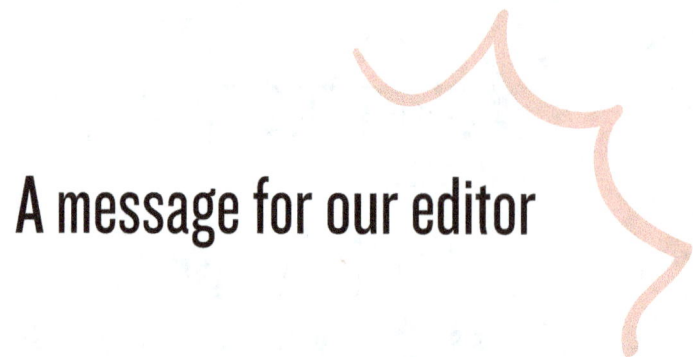

A message for our editor

Dear Valued Customer,

Your purchase just ignited a confetti cannon of joy in our headquarters!

You rock for choosing us, and we're seriously grateful for your support.
We get it, you're a discerning shopper, so having you pick us makes us do a happy dance.

We're always leveling up our products, services, and customer satisfaction, so your feedback is gold dust. If you have a sec, a review would make our day!

Got questions? We're here to help, rain or shine.

Thanks again for making our world brighter! See you soon with even more awesome stuff!

Sincerely,

Braulio Cabrera - Aura Editions

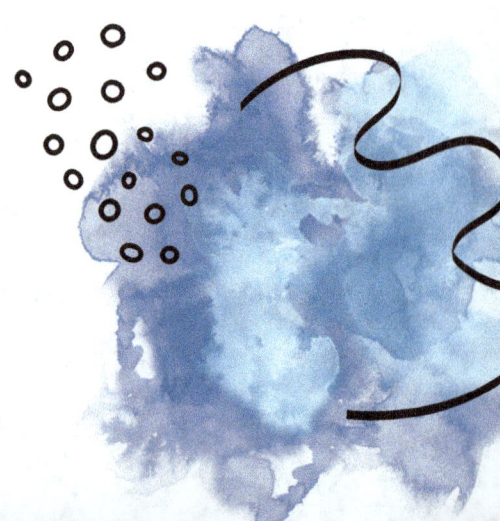

INKSPIRATION STATION

Here are a few ideas to get you started:

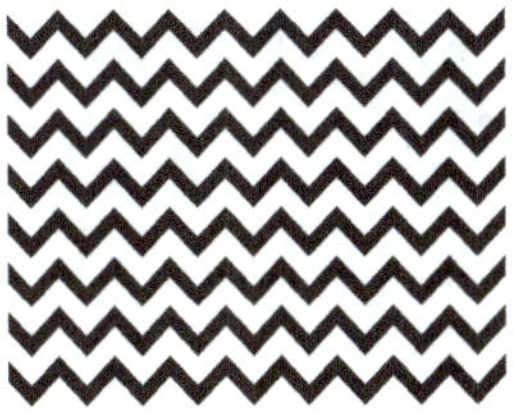

Zig zag lines

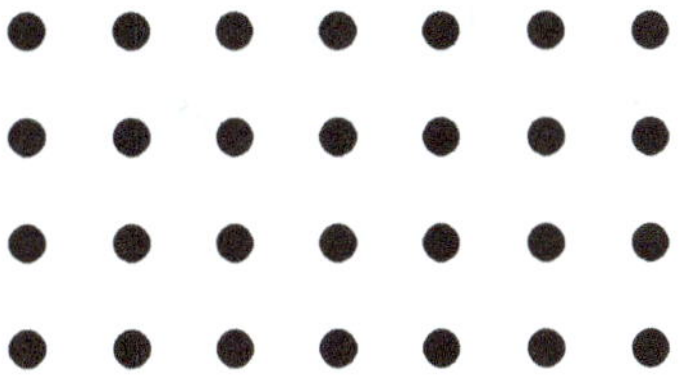

Dots

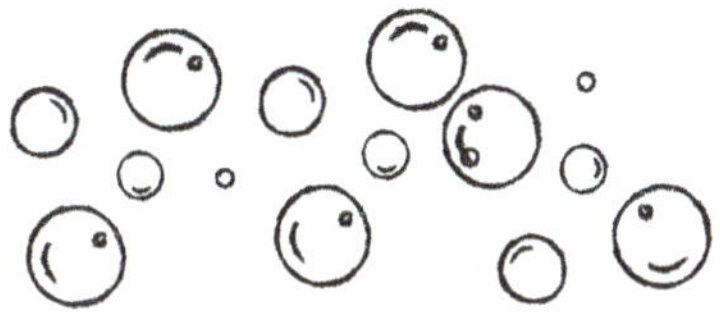

Bubbles

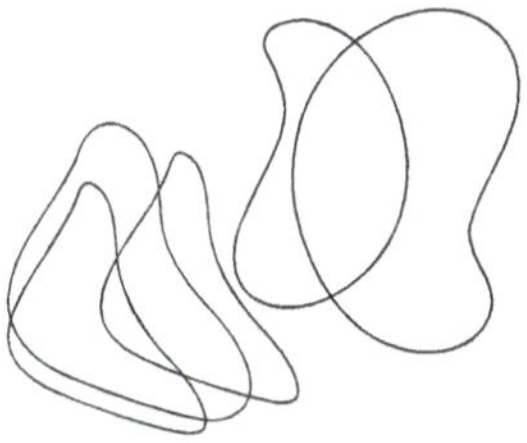

Organic shapes

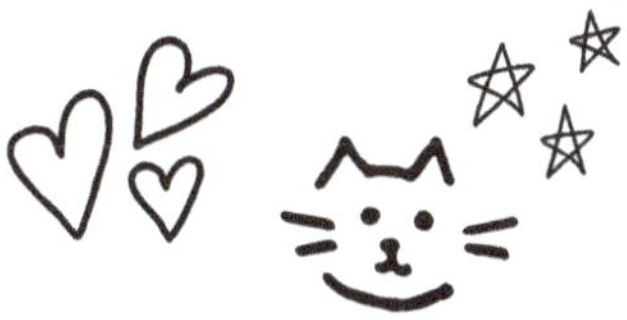

Random drawings

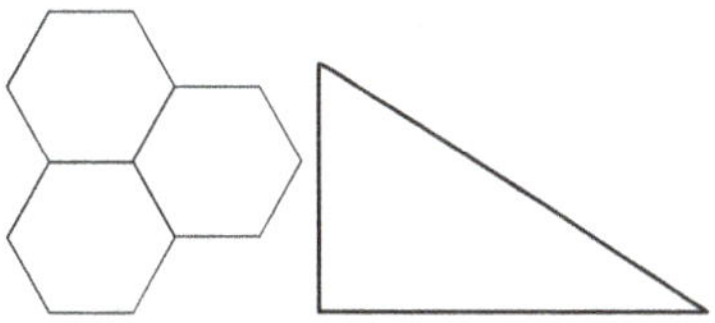

Geometric shapes

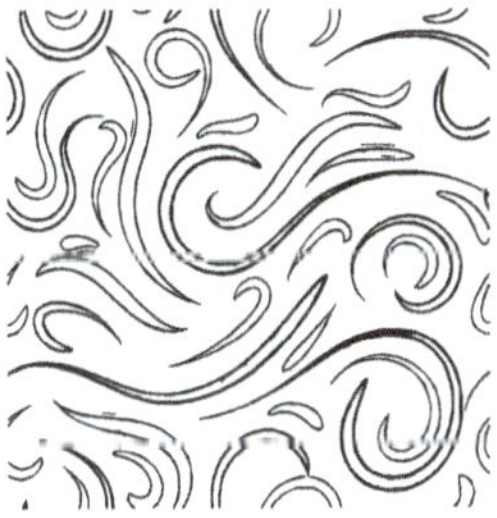

Swirls

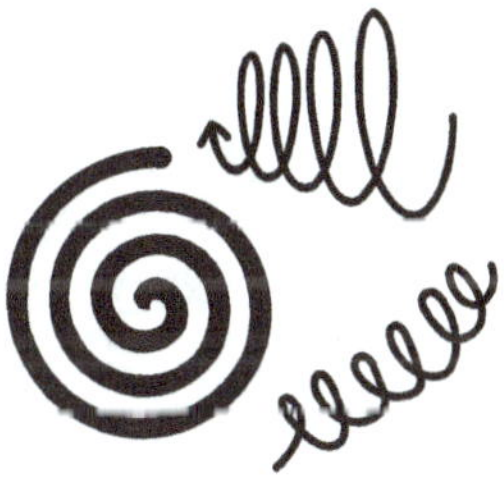

Spirals

- Design a pattern or texture.
- Draw a landscape or cityscape.
- Just doodle and see what happens!

No matter what you create, be sure to have fun and let your creativity flow.

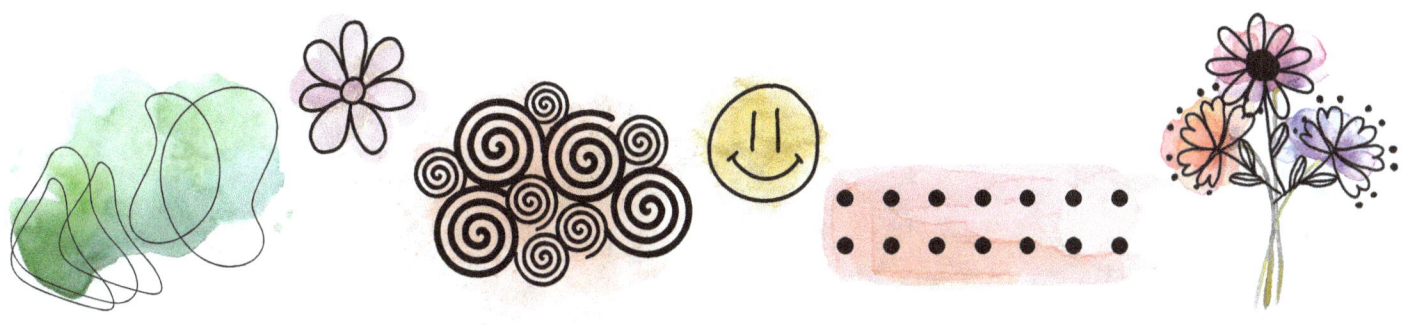

IT'S TIME TO
Experiment with your own inkspiration!

Let your imagination run wild on this blank page!
Explore different pen thicknesses, create patterns, and doodle to your heart's content. Use this page to experiment with different techniques and find your own unique style. **The possibilities are endless!**

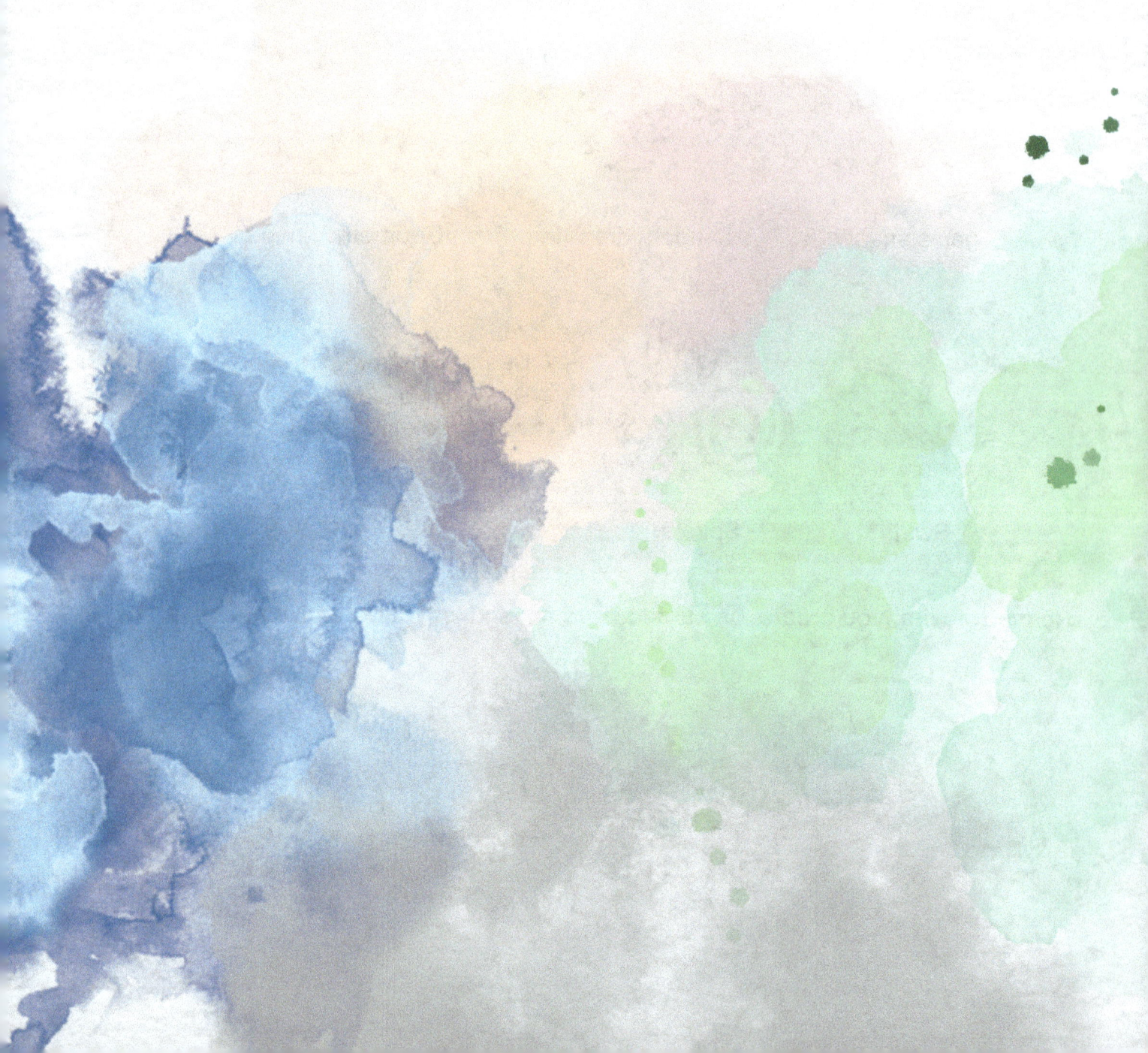

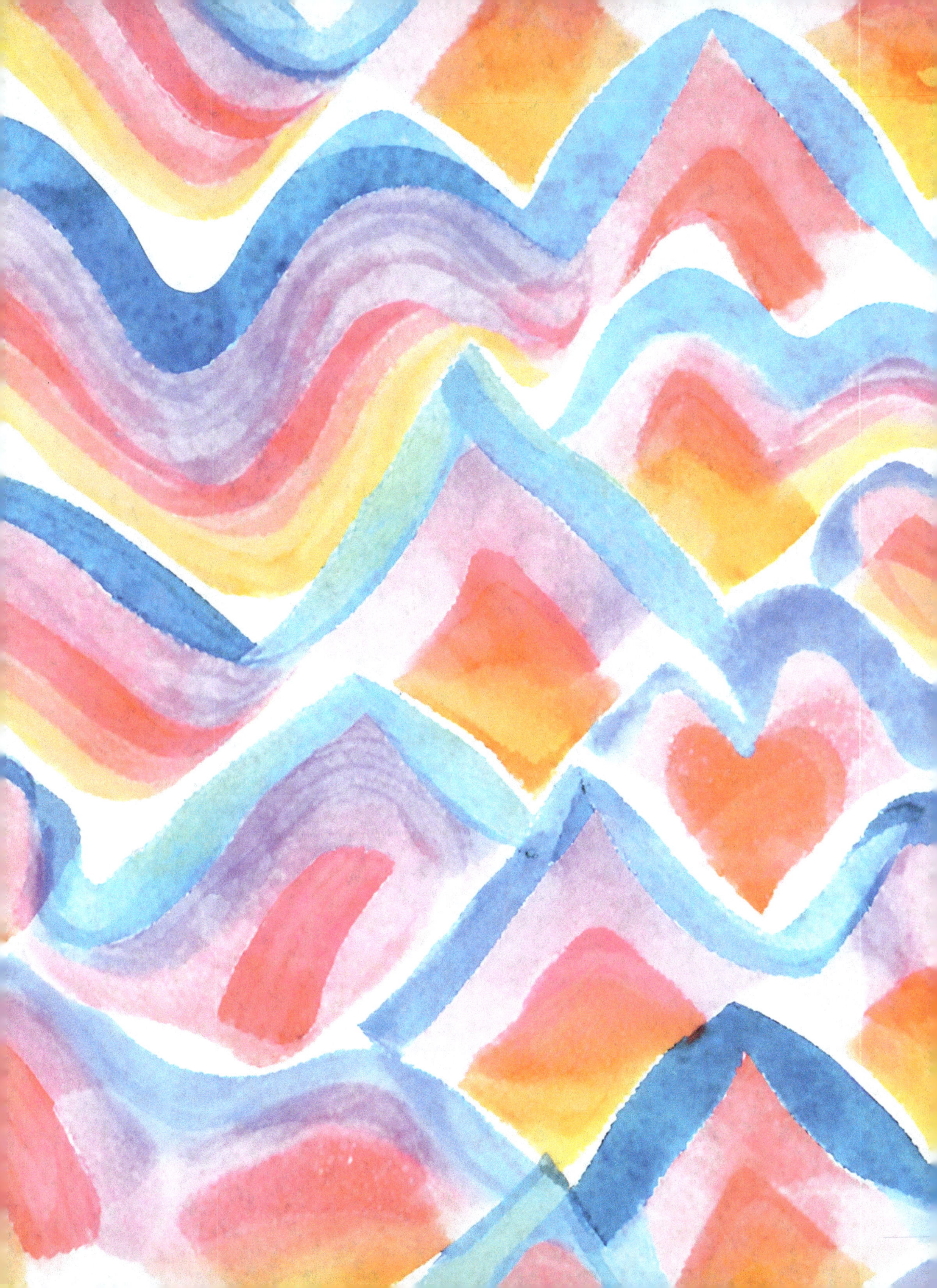

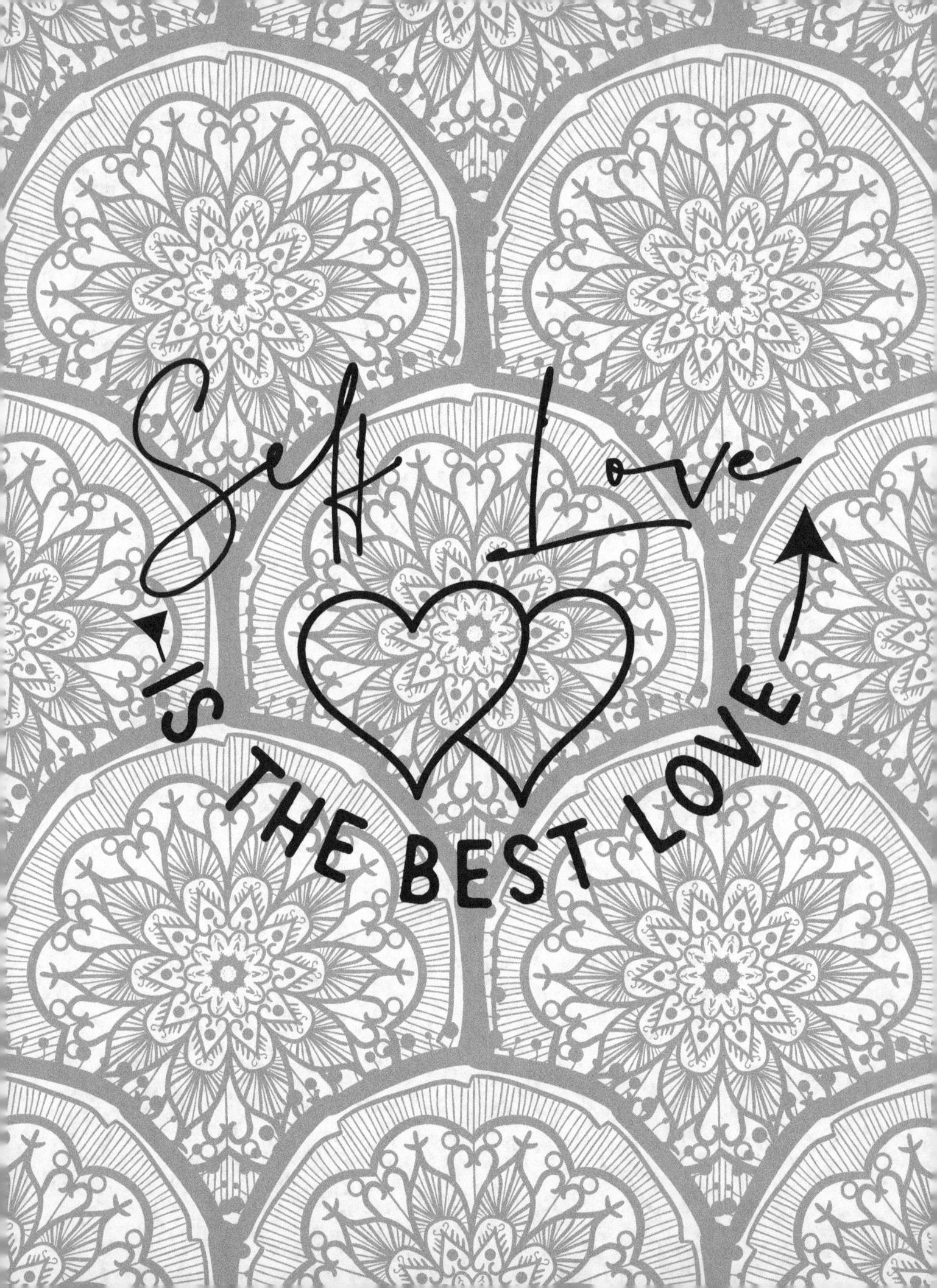

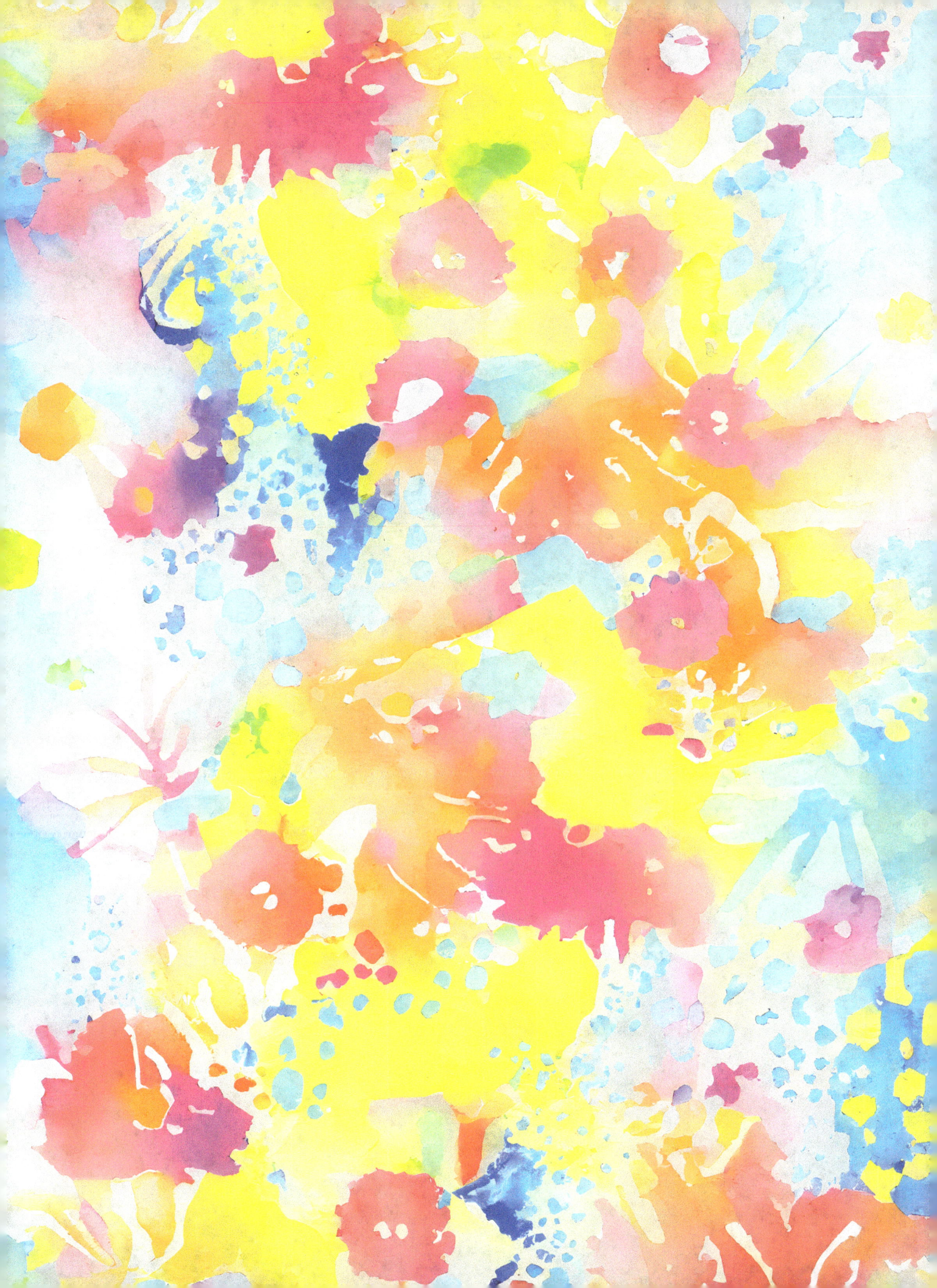

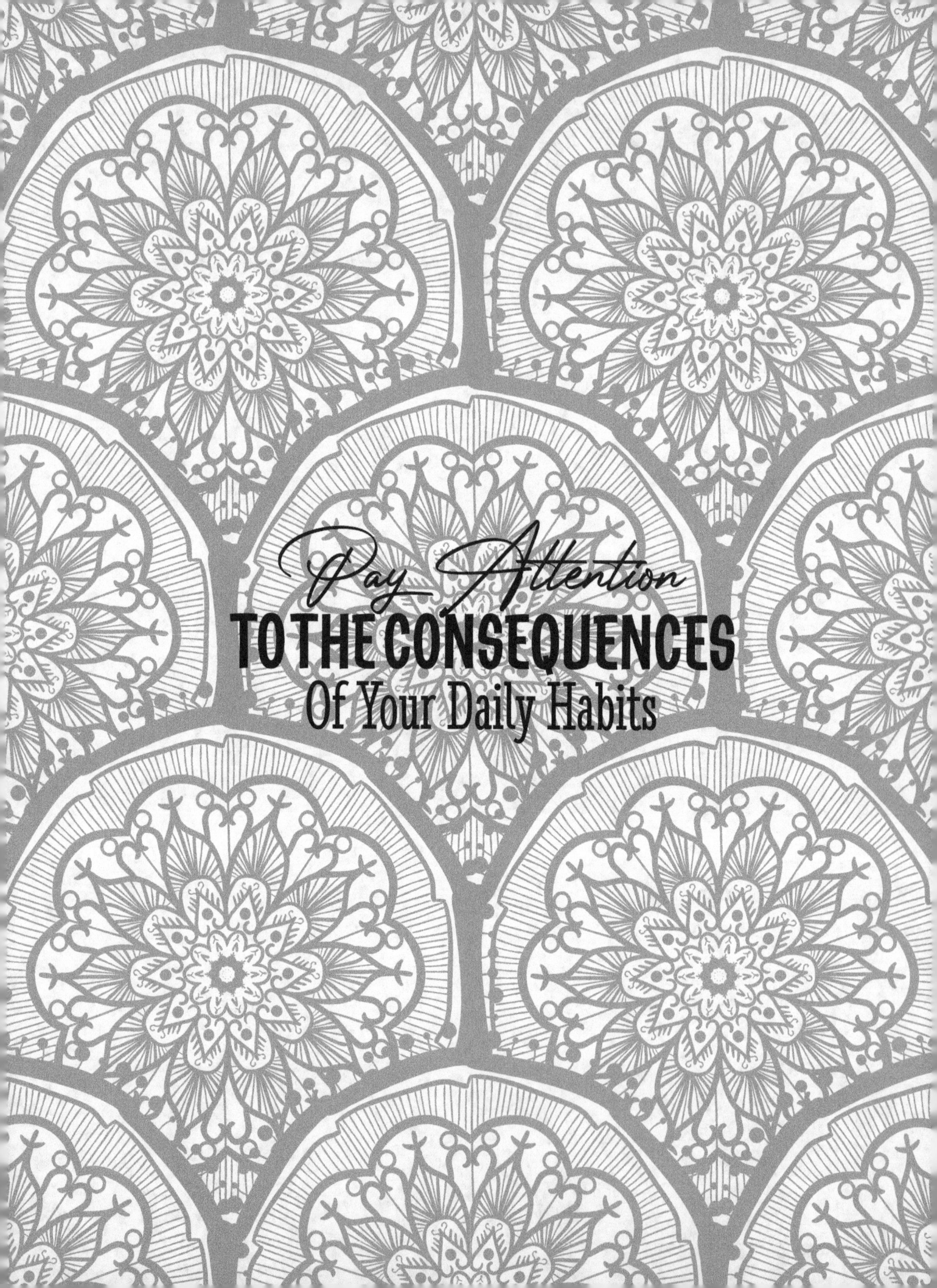

Pay Attention
TO THE CONSEQUENCES
Of Your Daily Habits

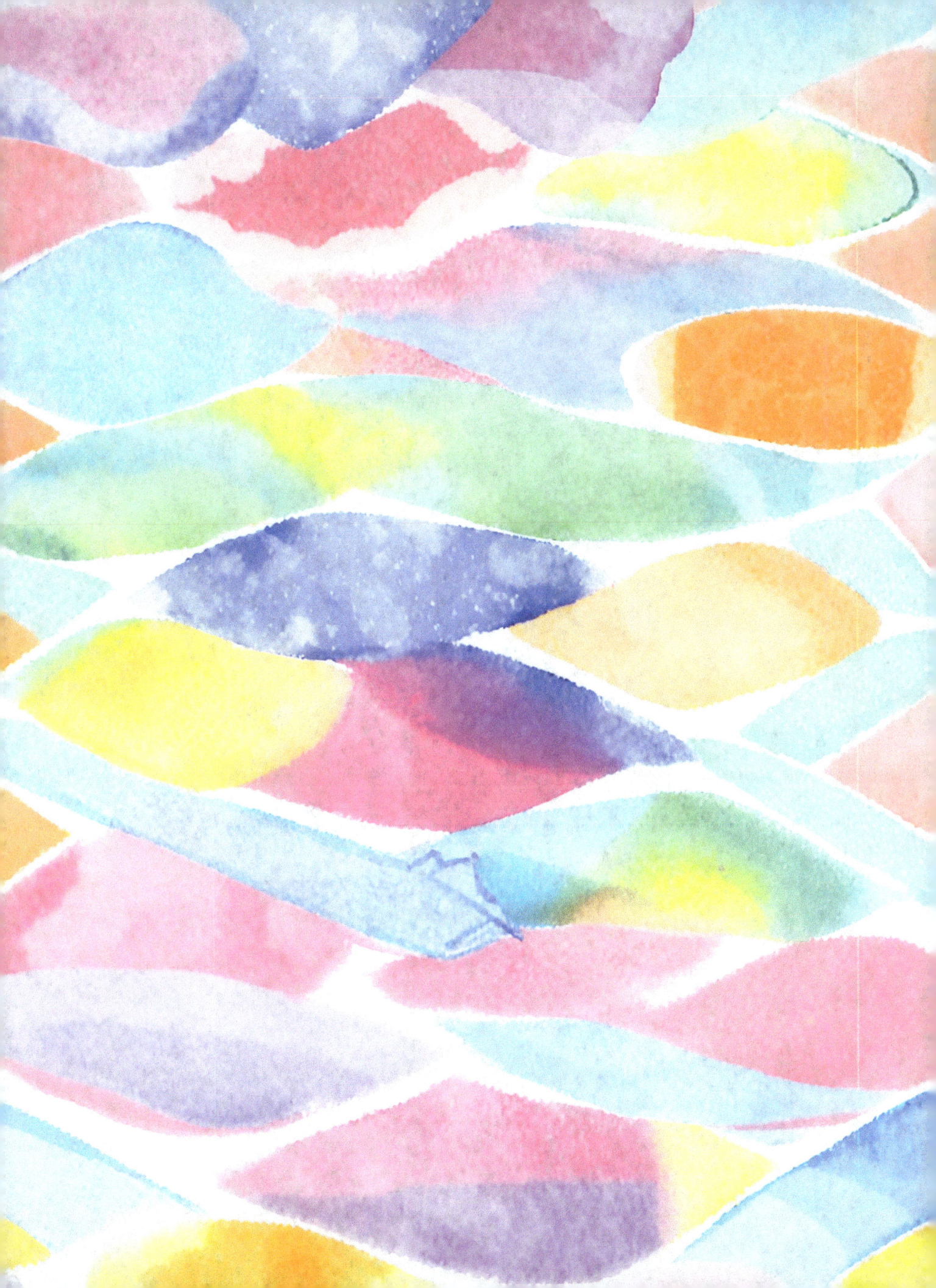

GO FORTH AND BE FIERCE

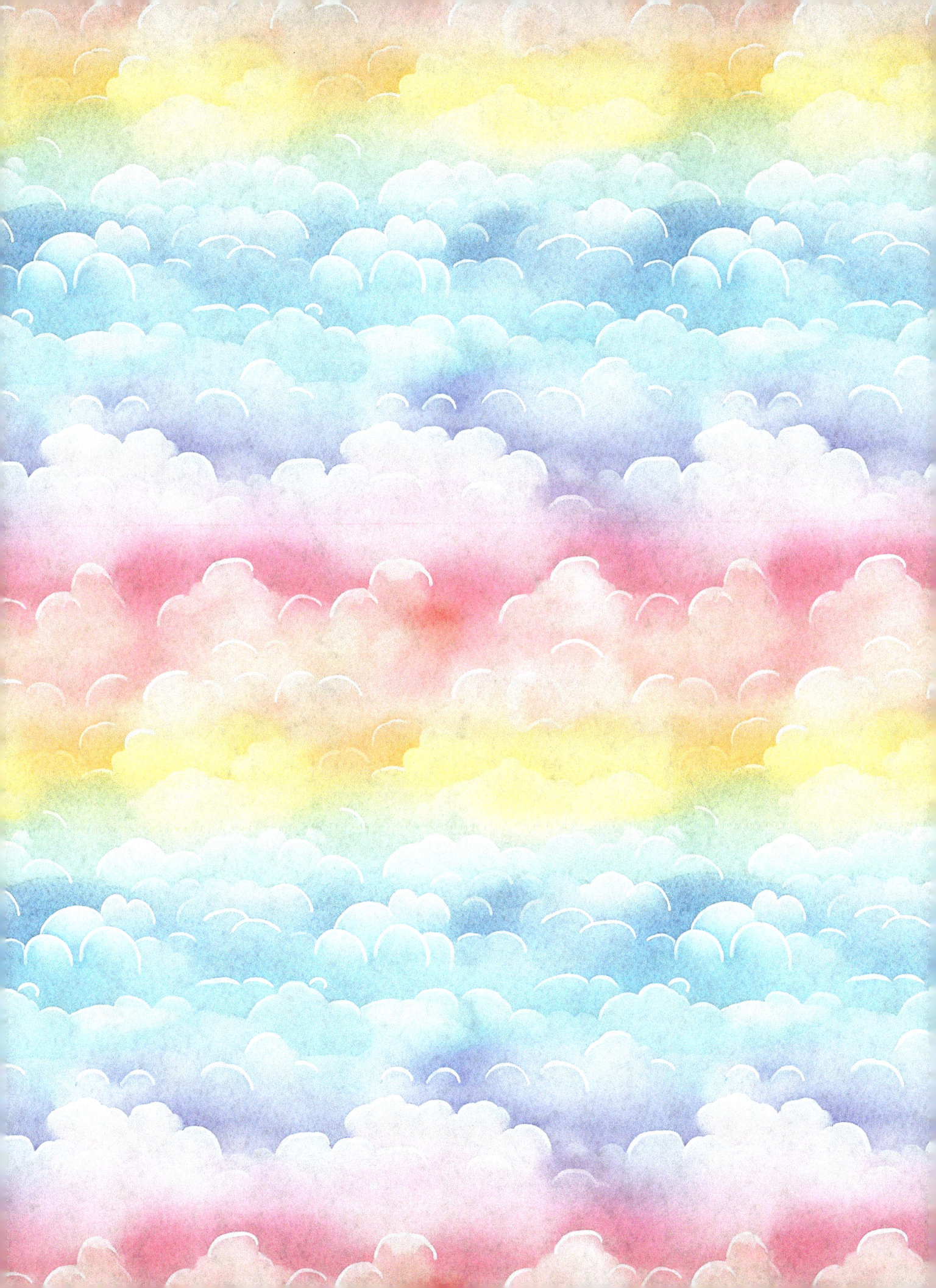

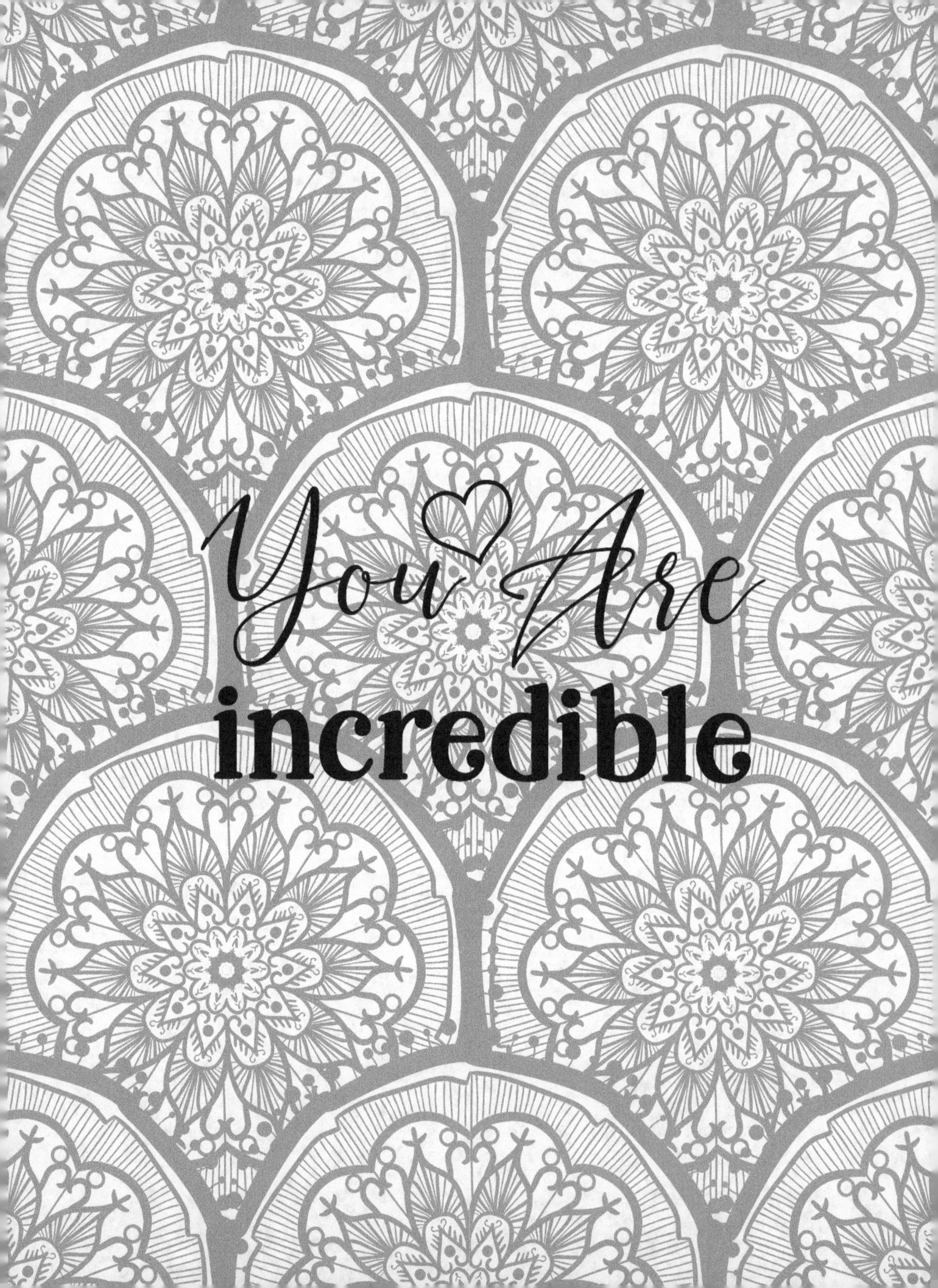

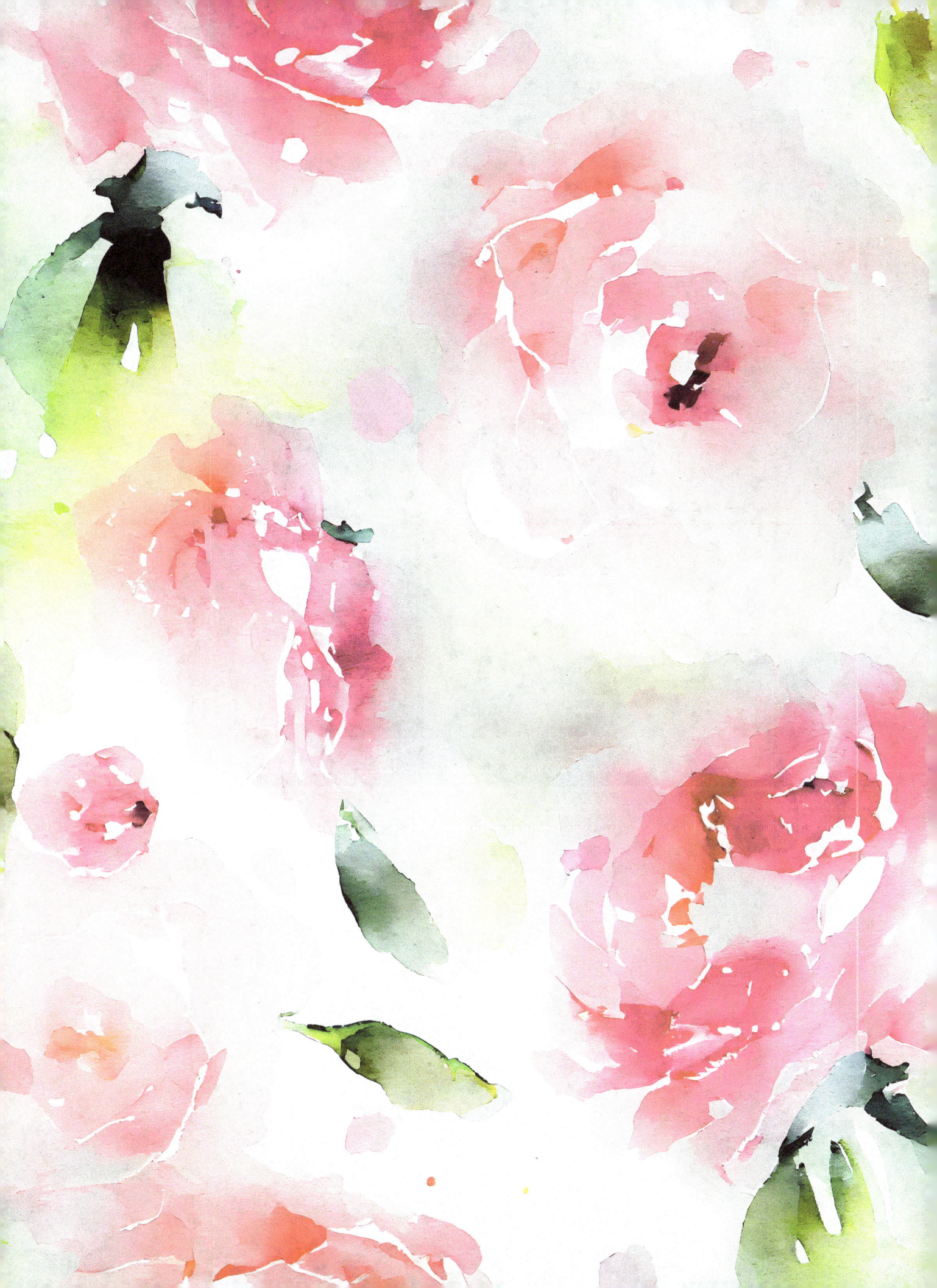

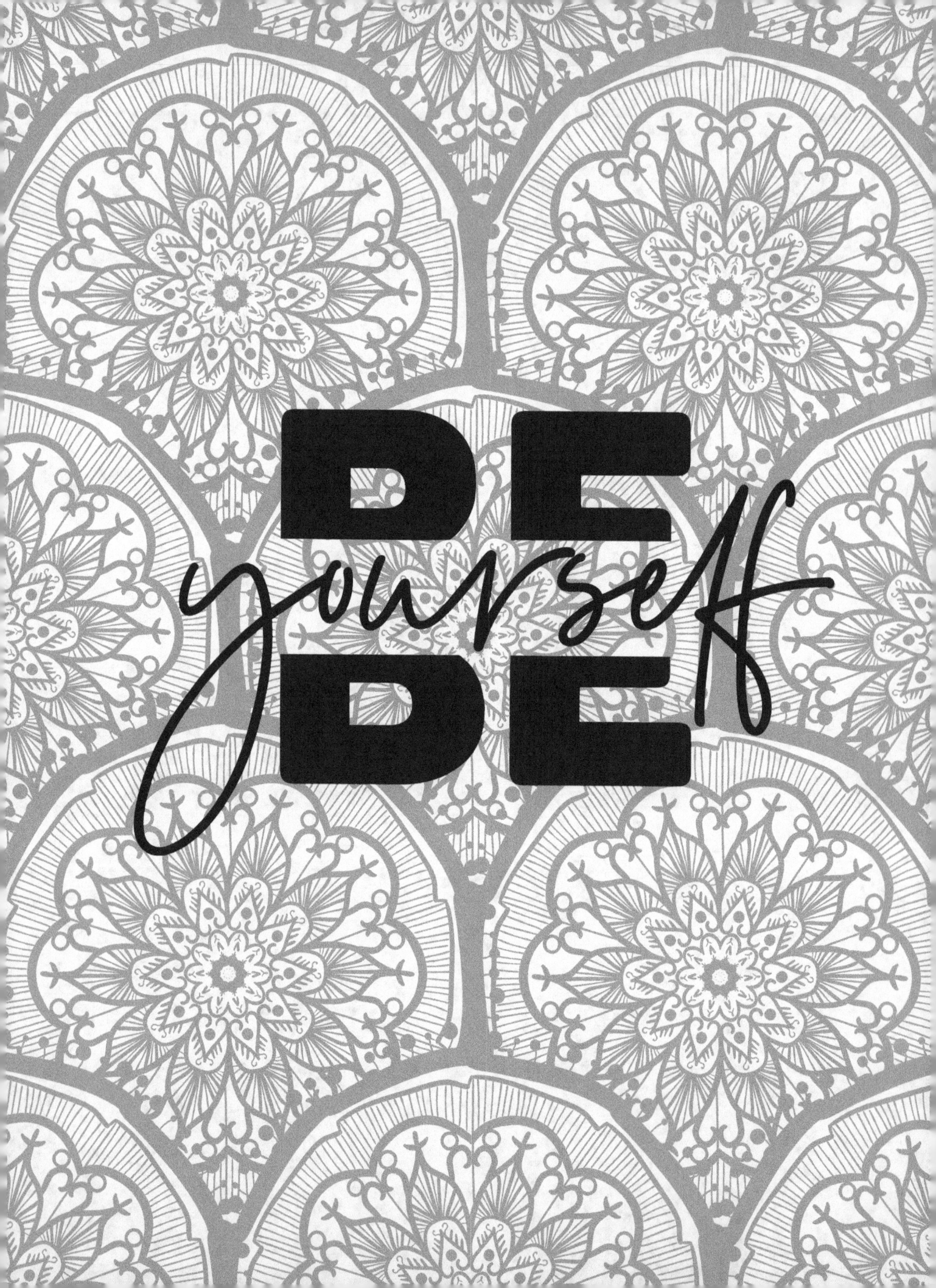

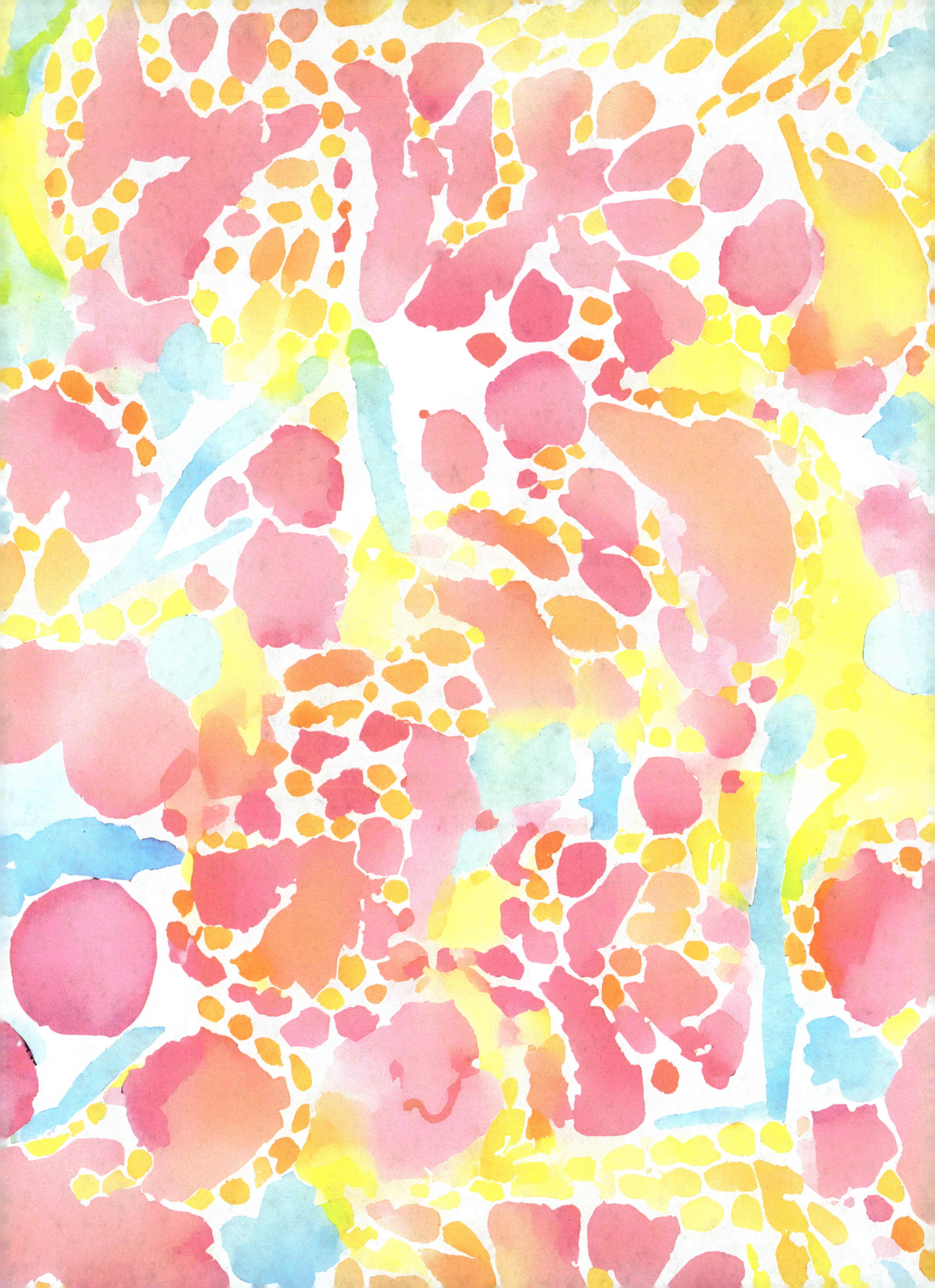

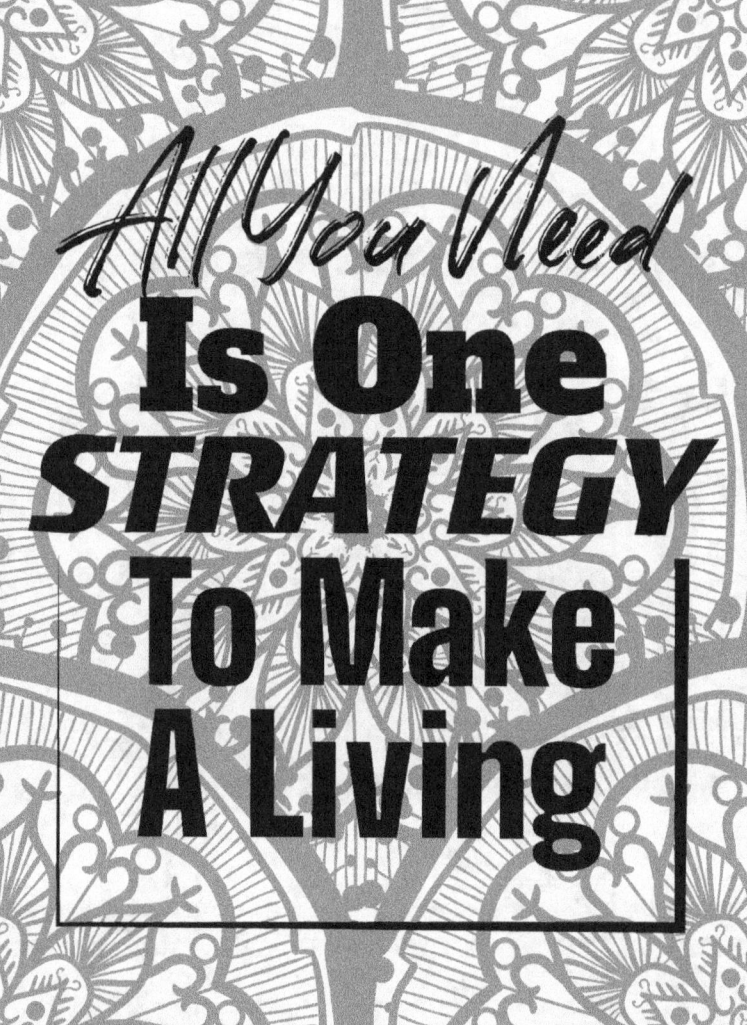

All You Need **Is One STRATEGY To Make A Living**

PERFECTLY Imperfect

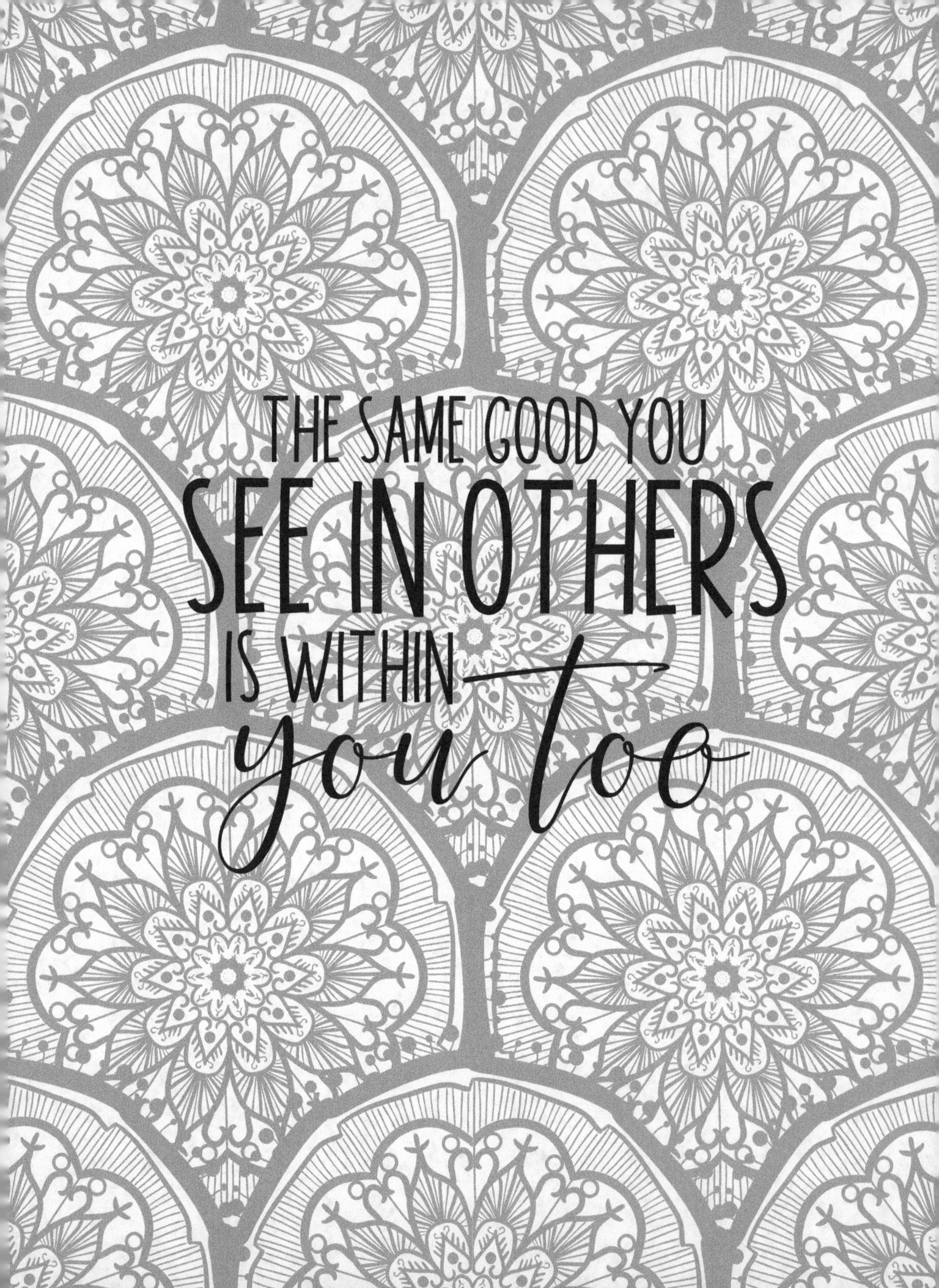

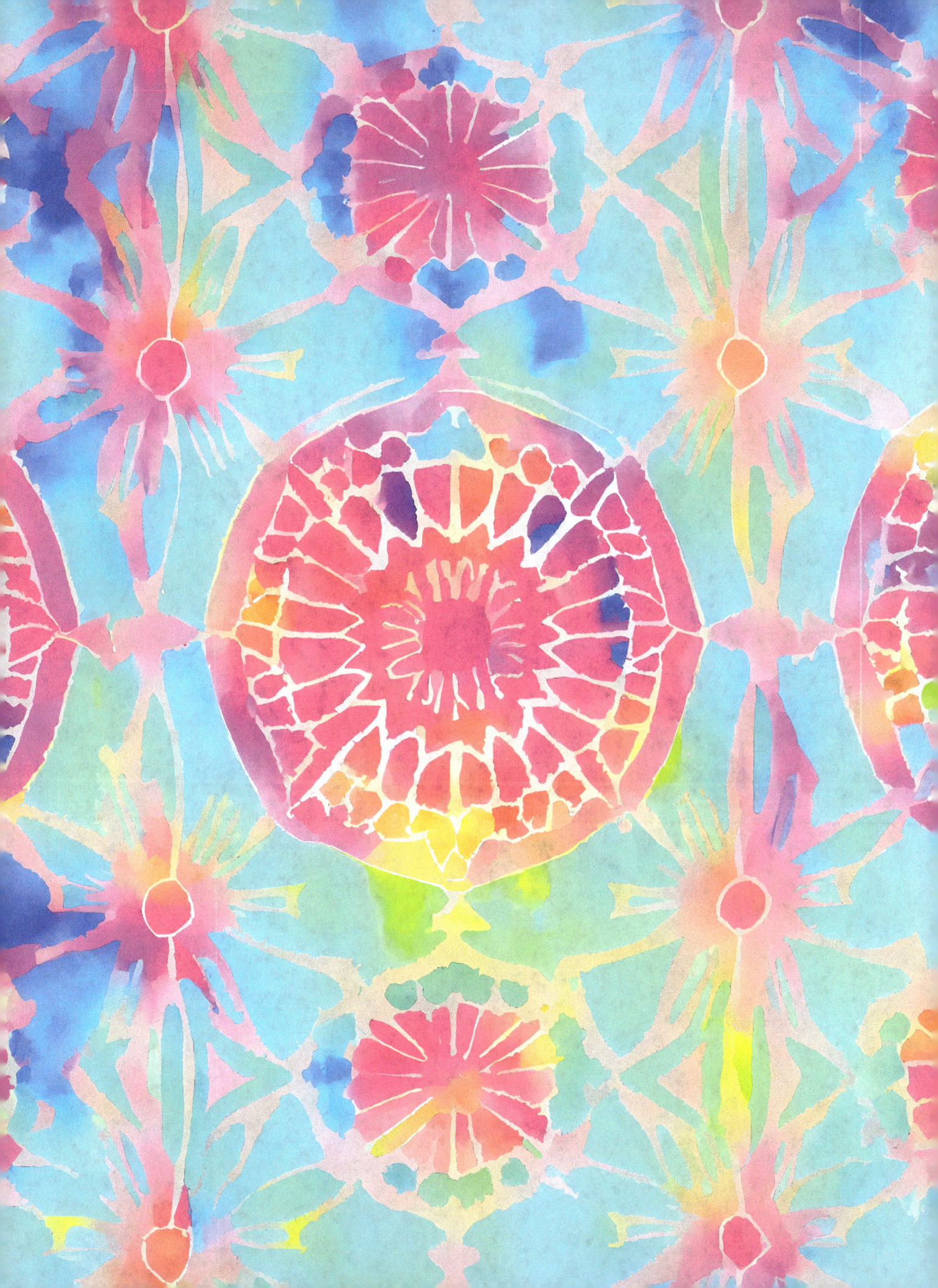

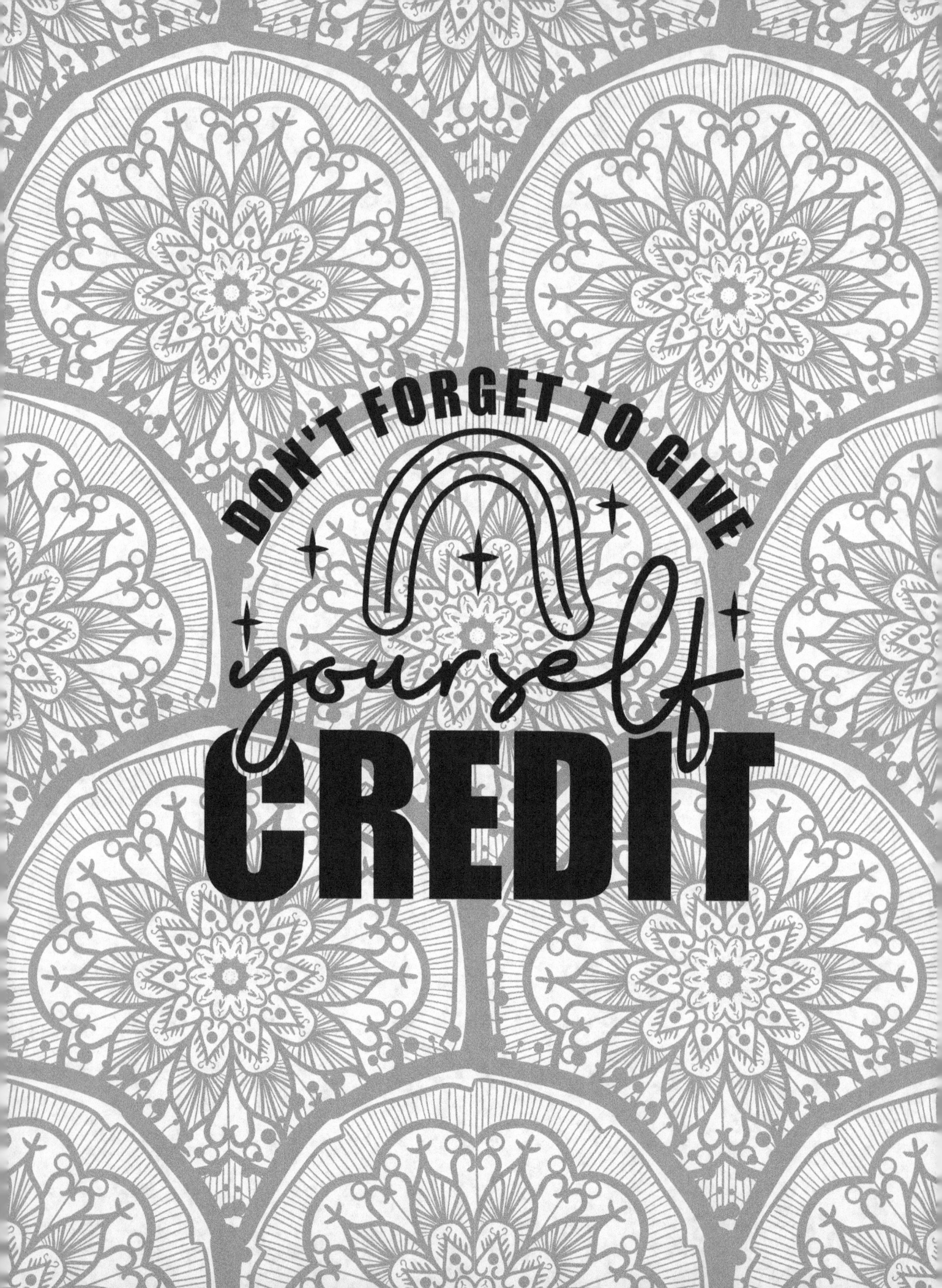

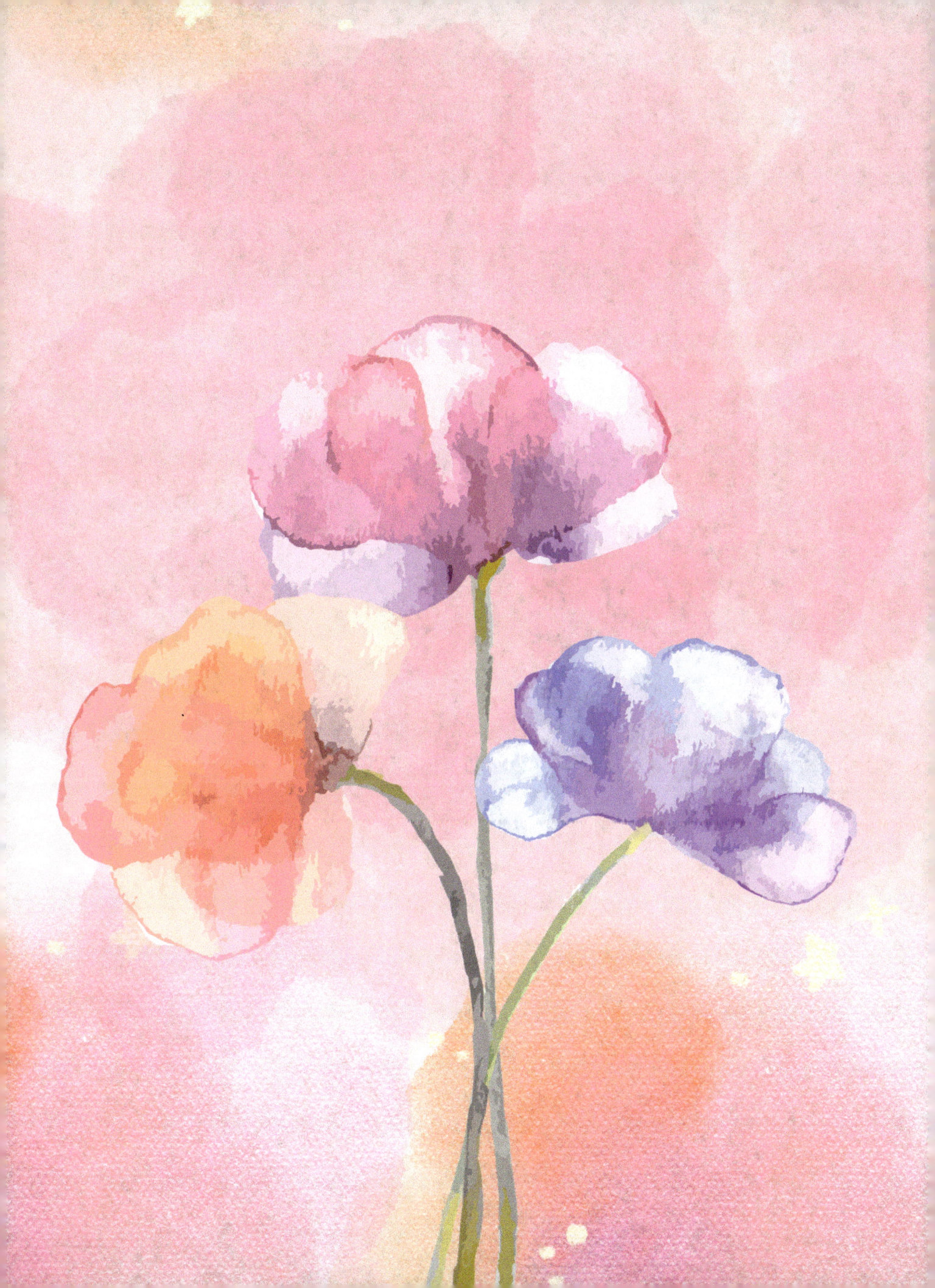

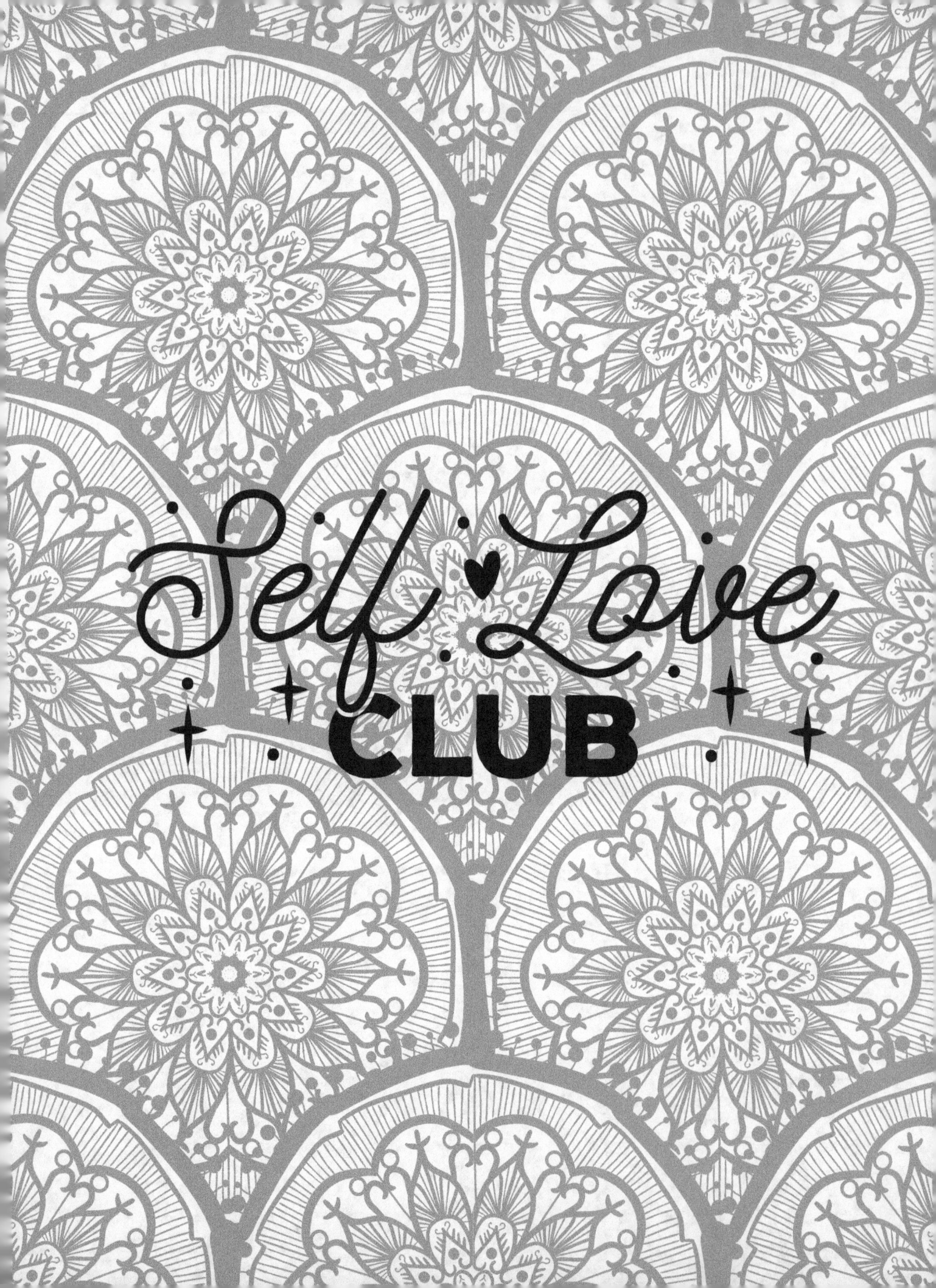

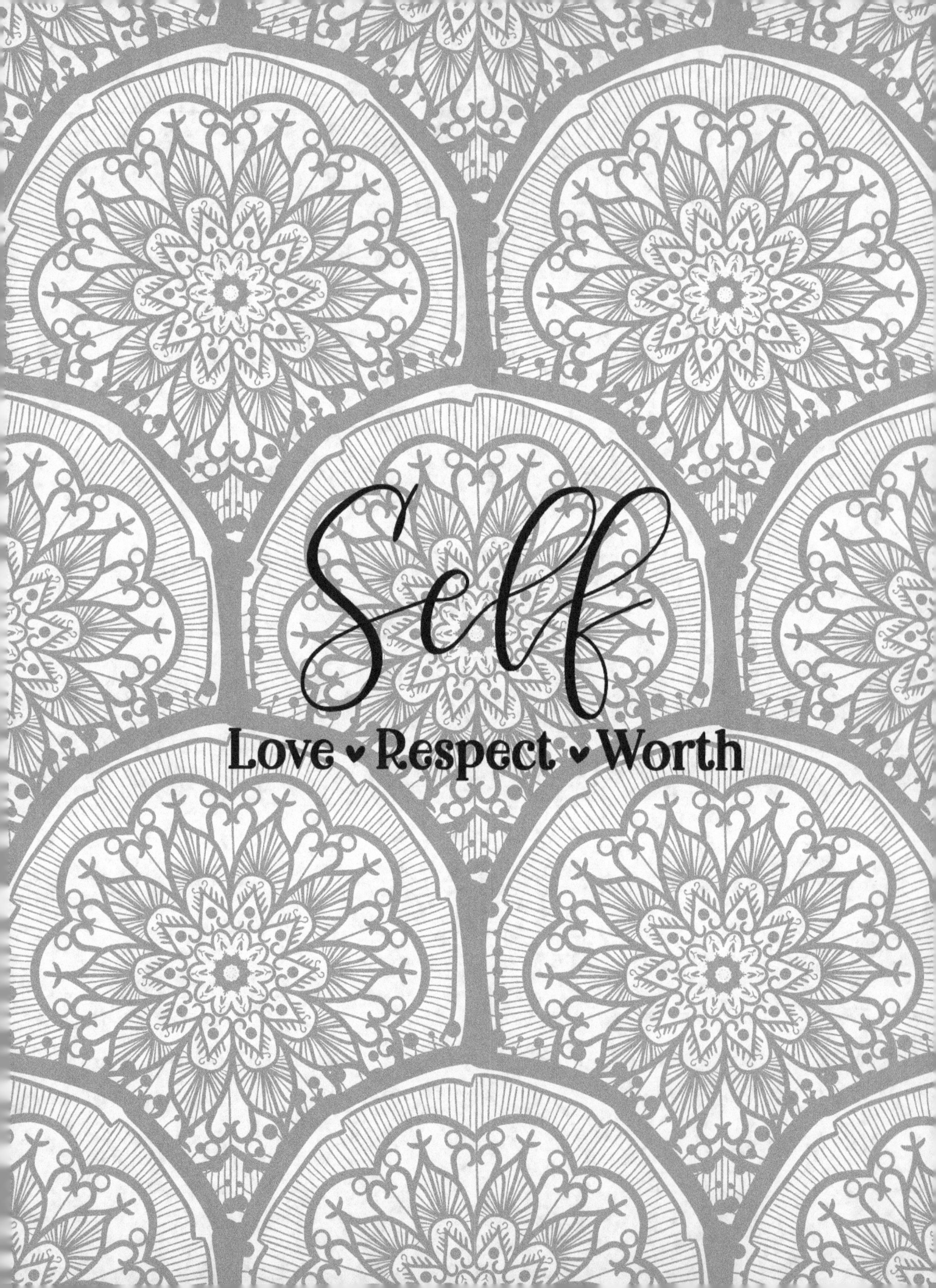

Self

Love ♥ Respect ♥ Worth

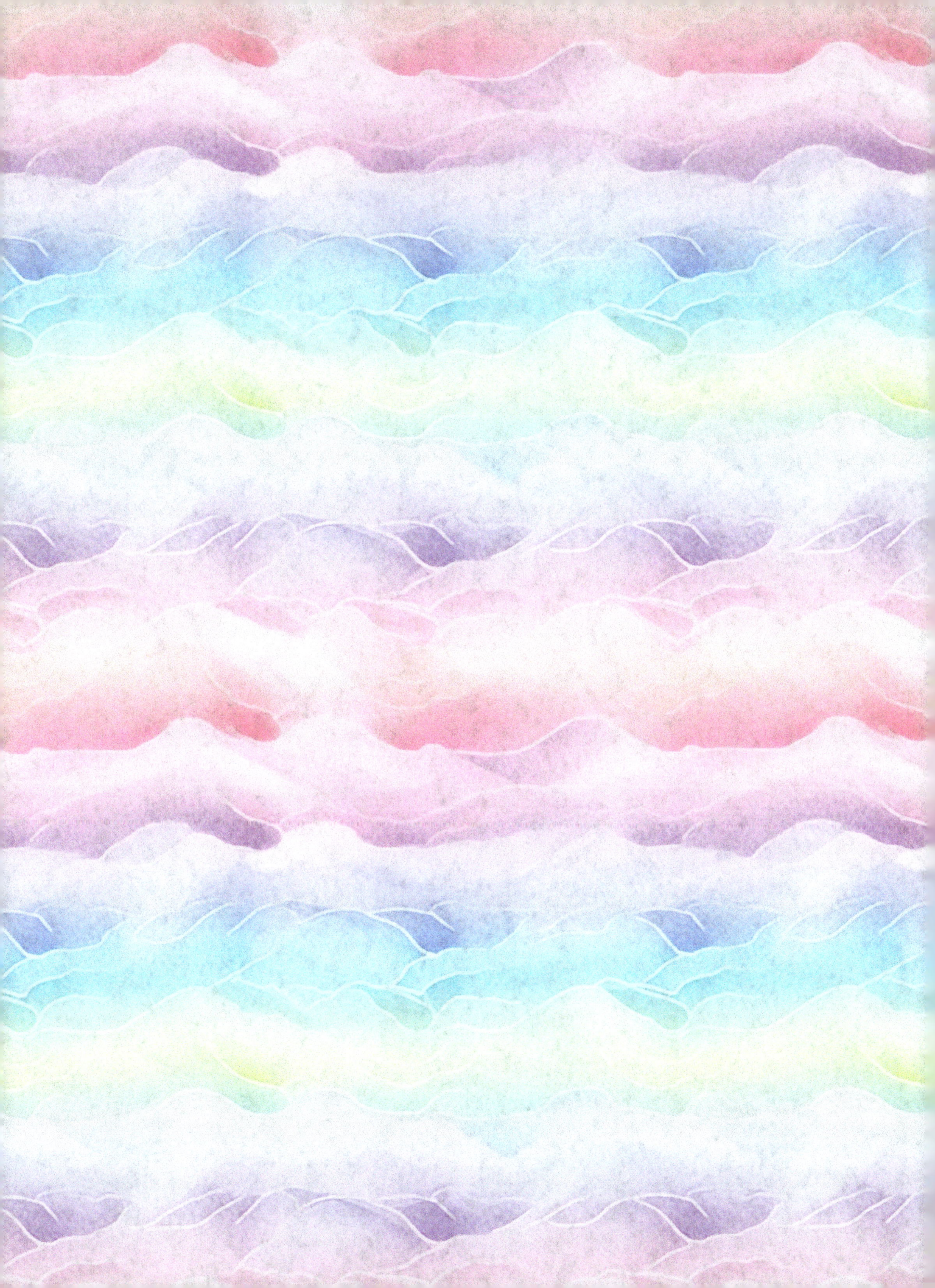

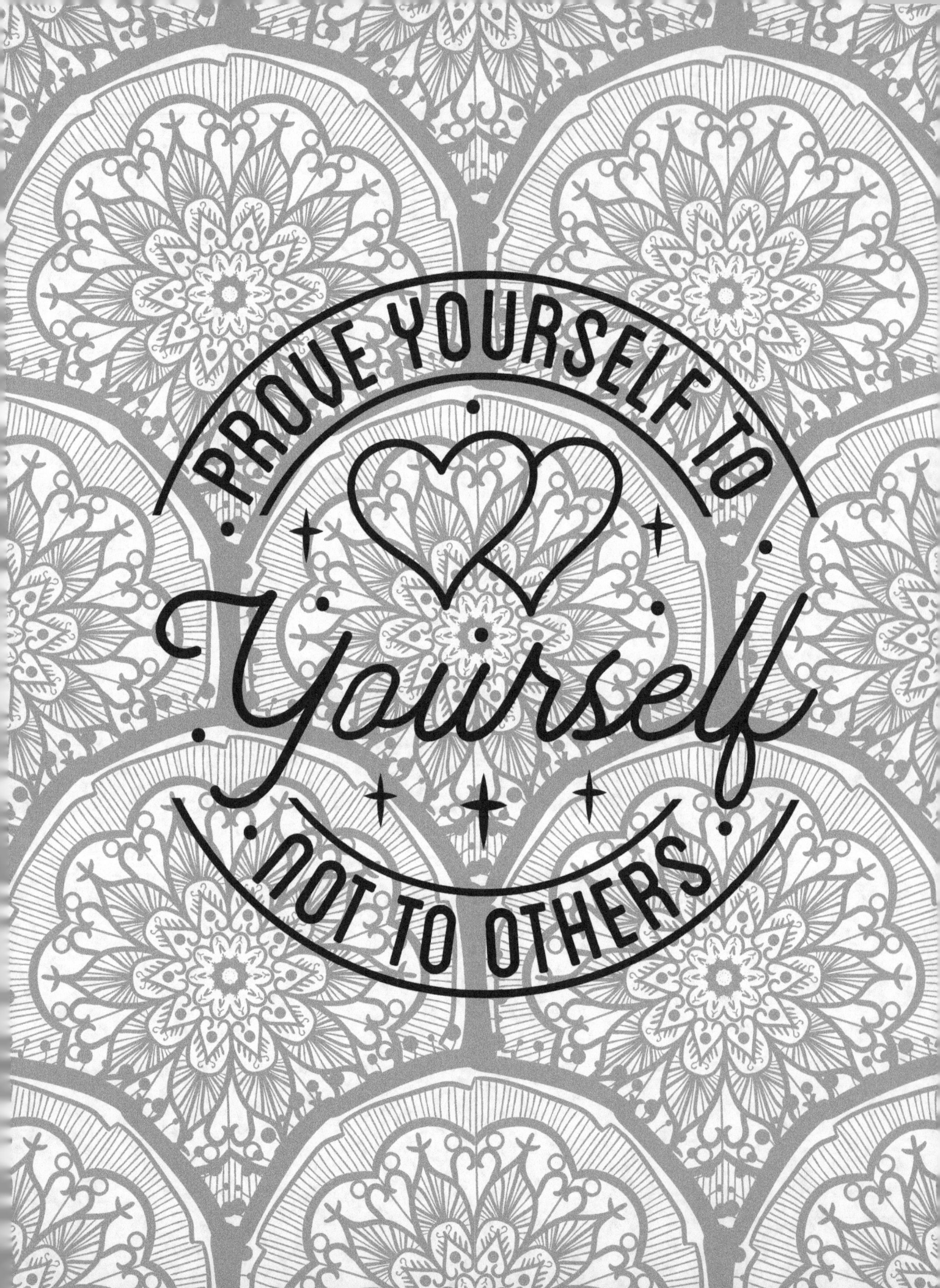

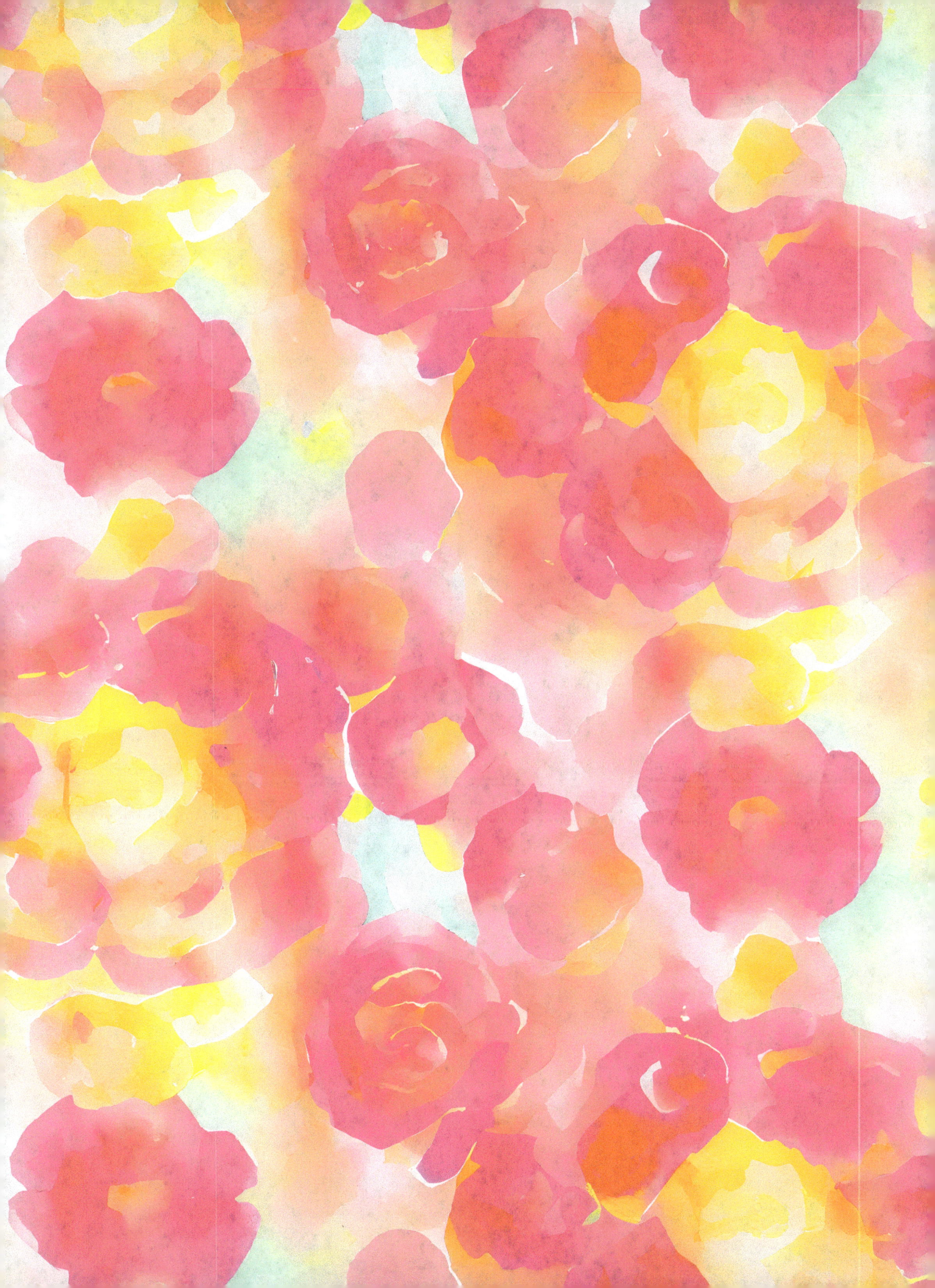

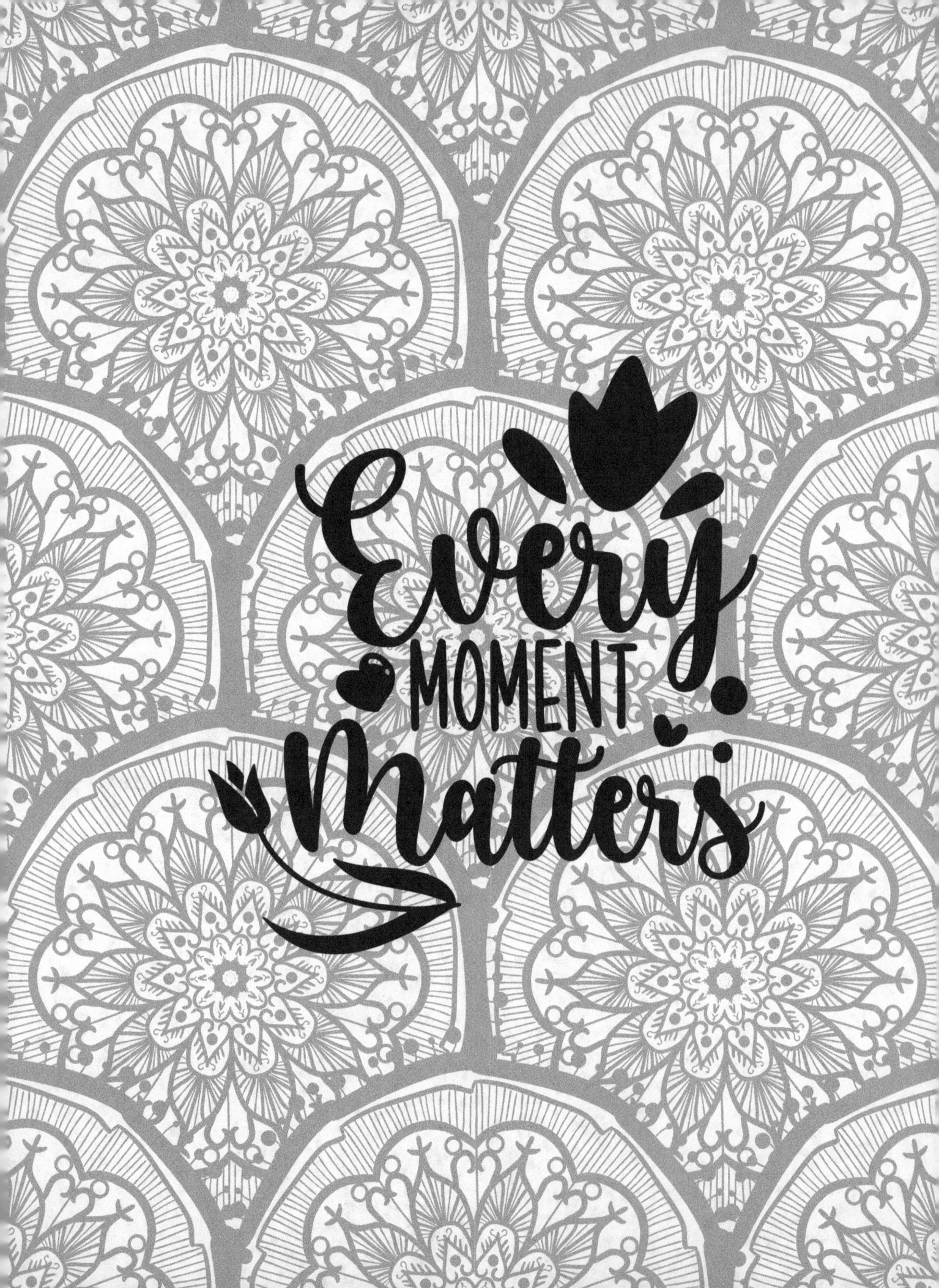

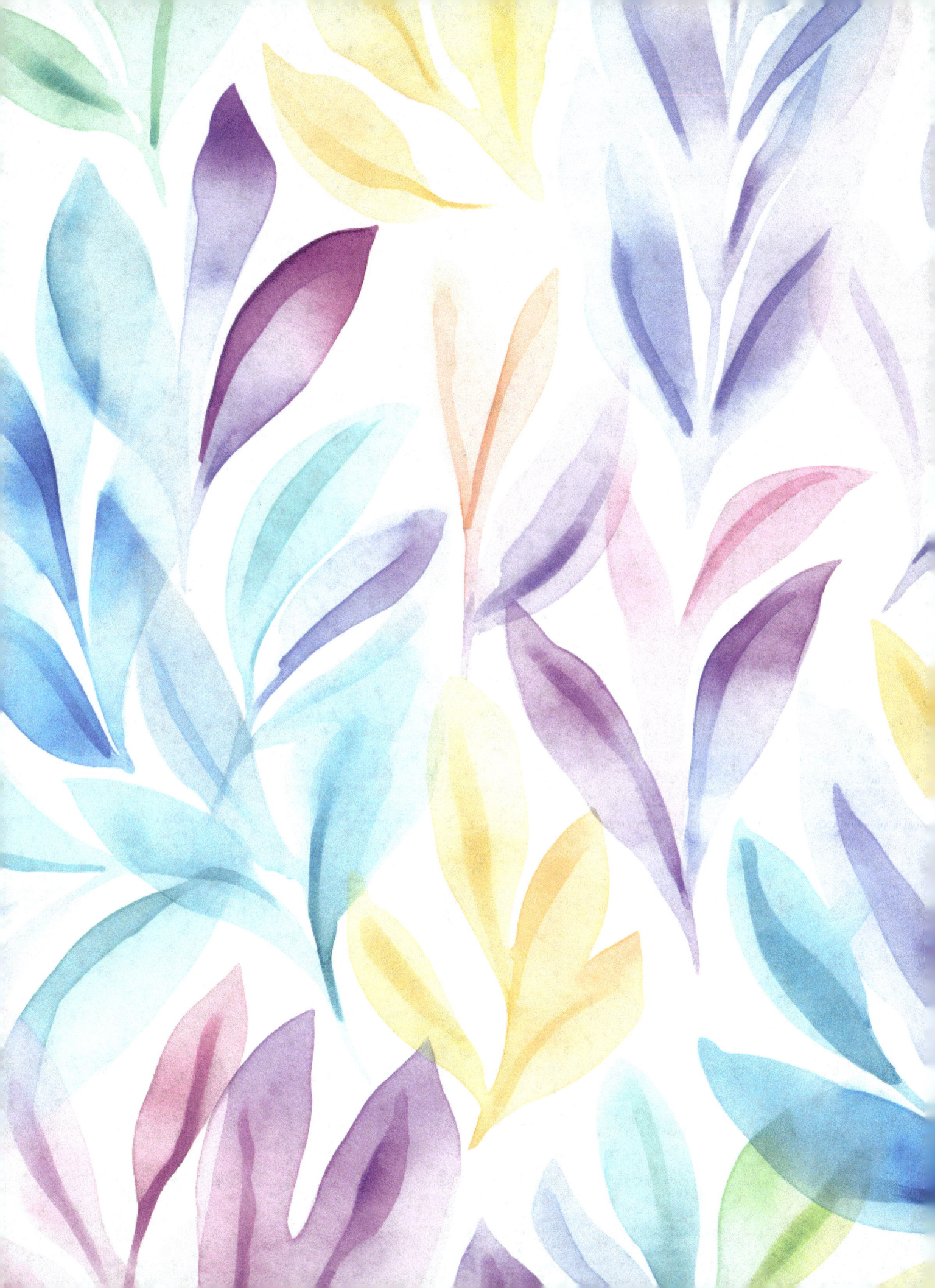

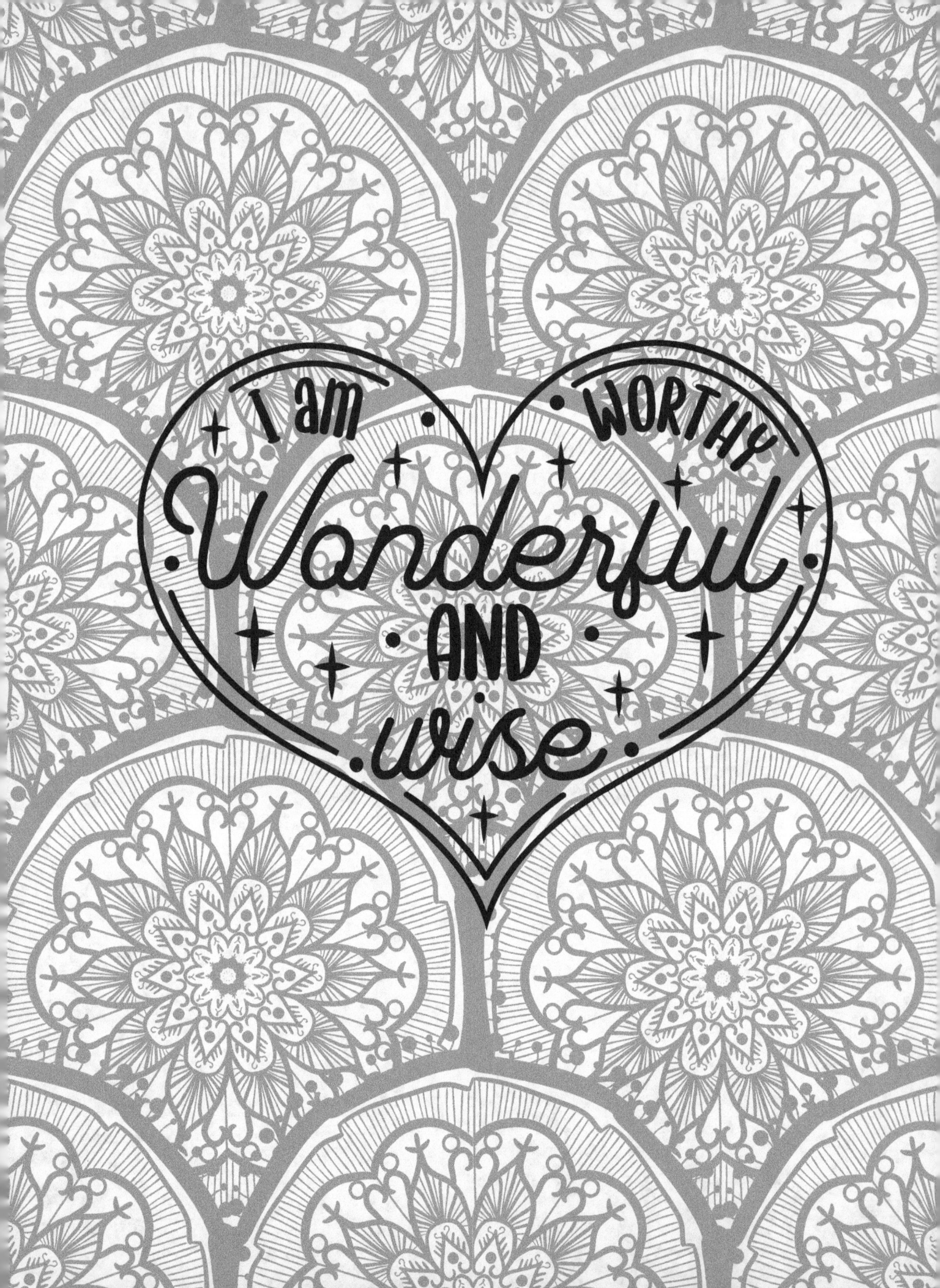

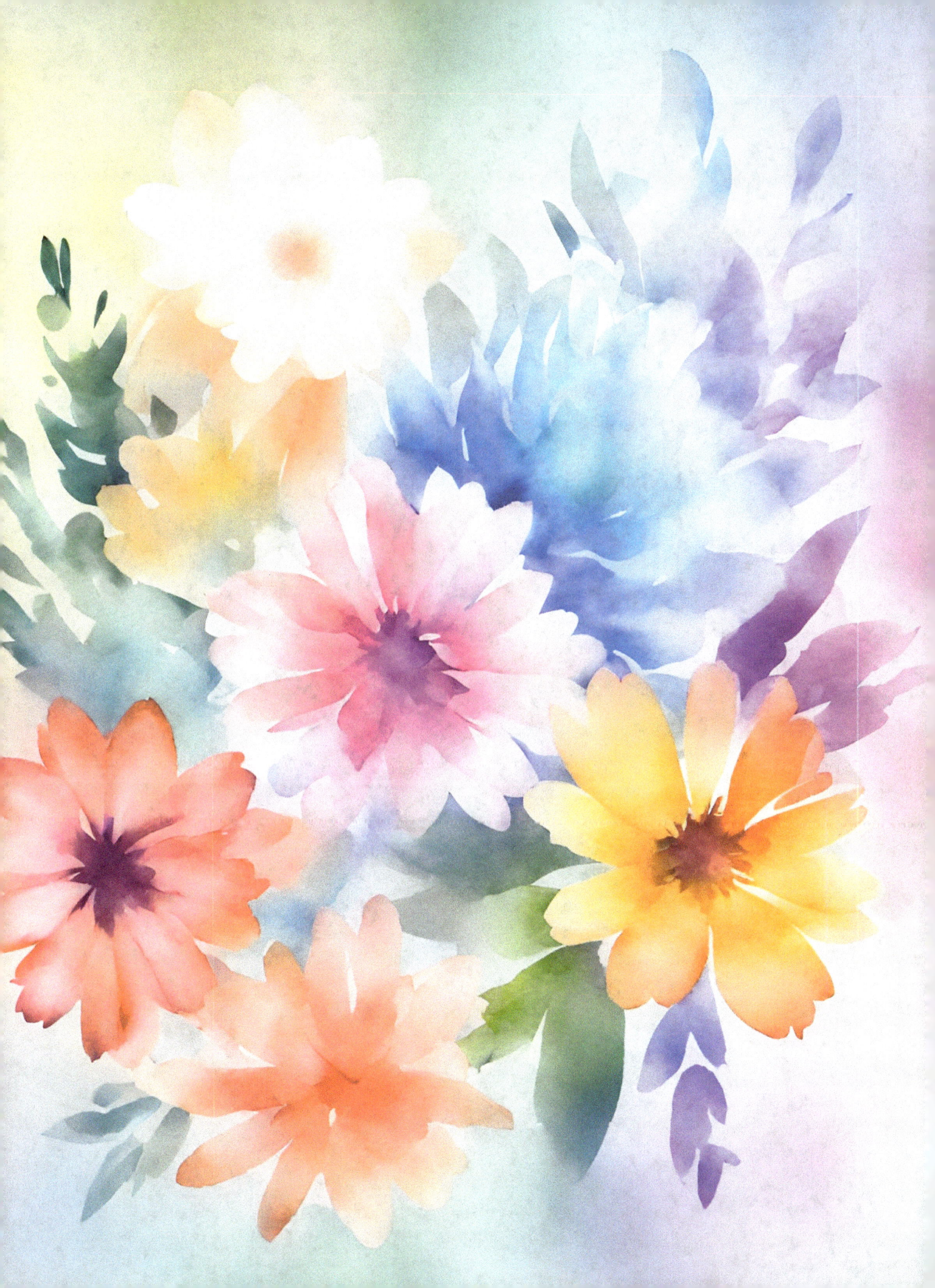

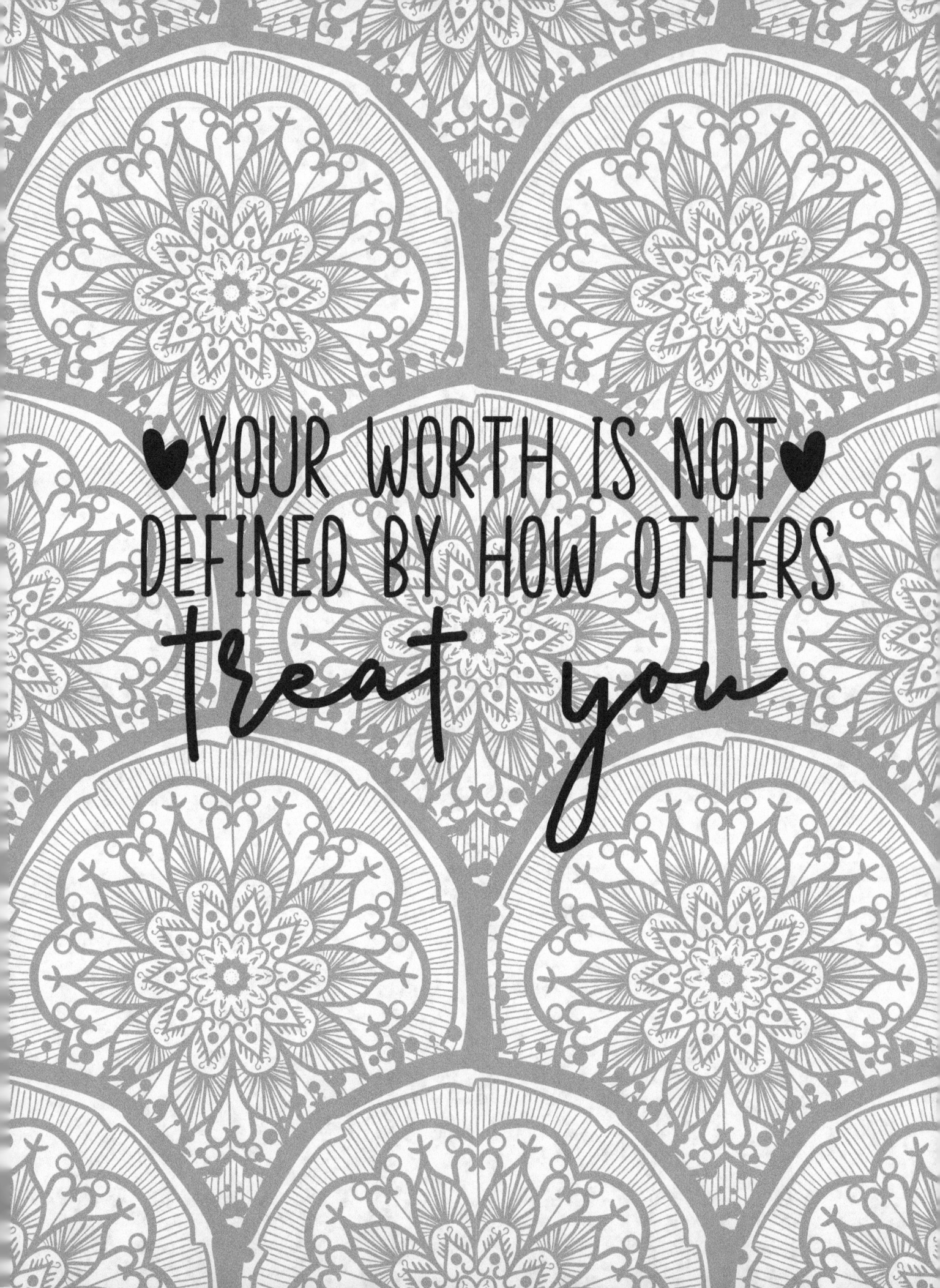

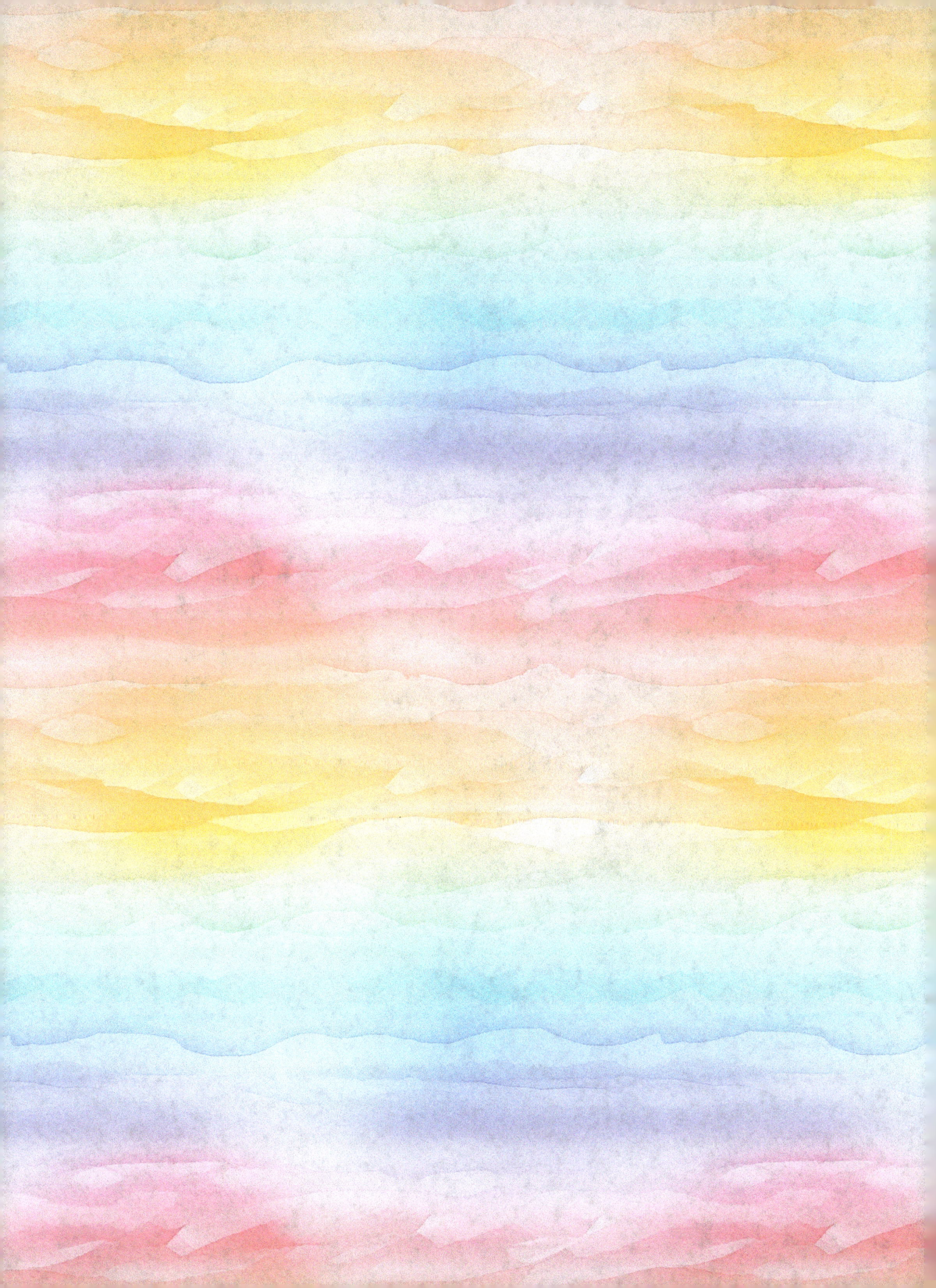

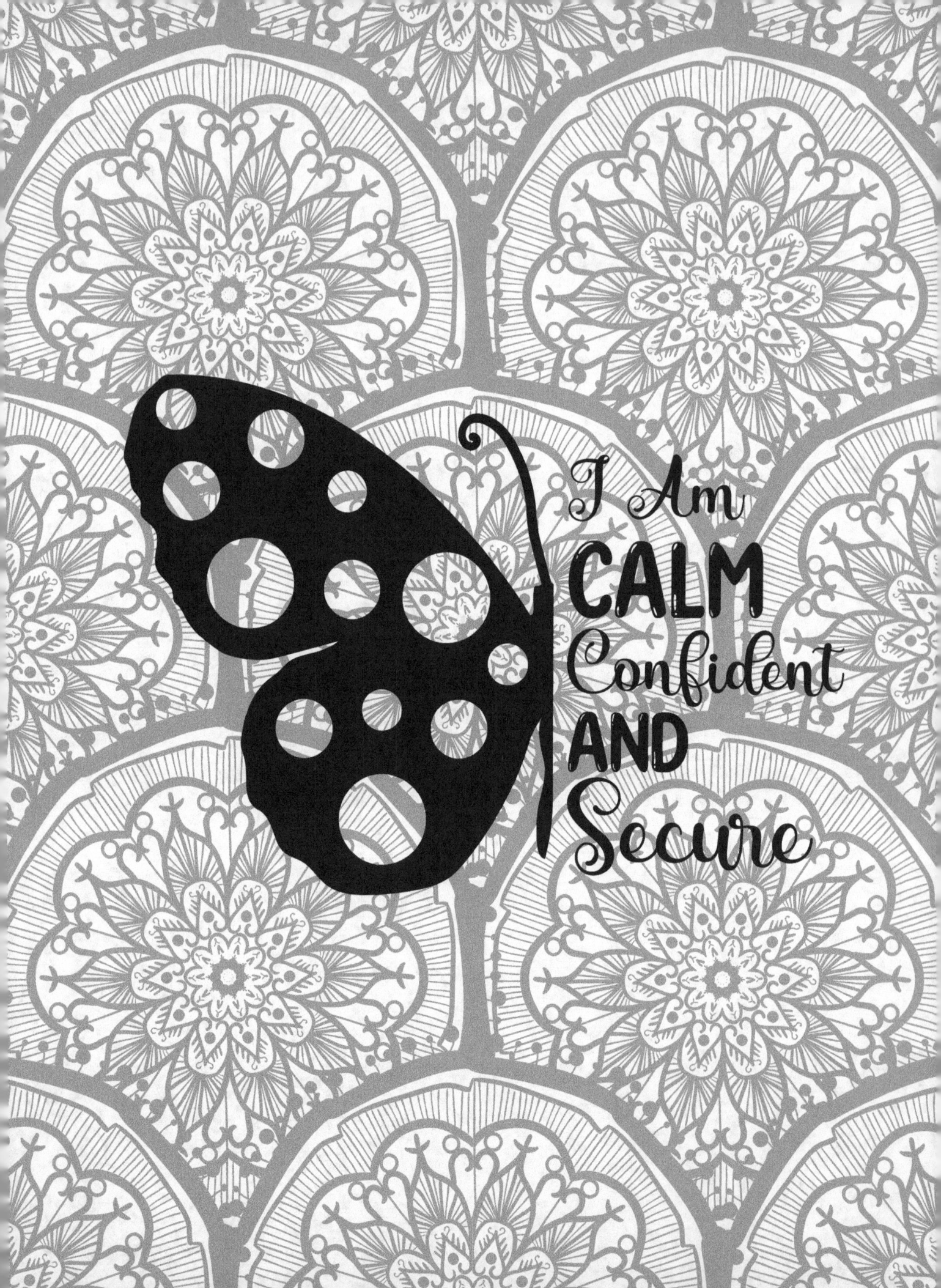

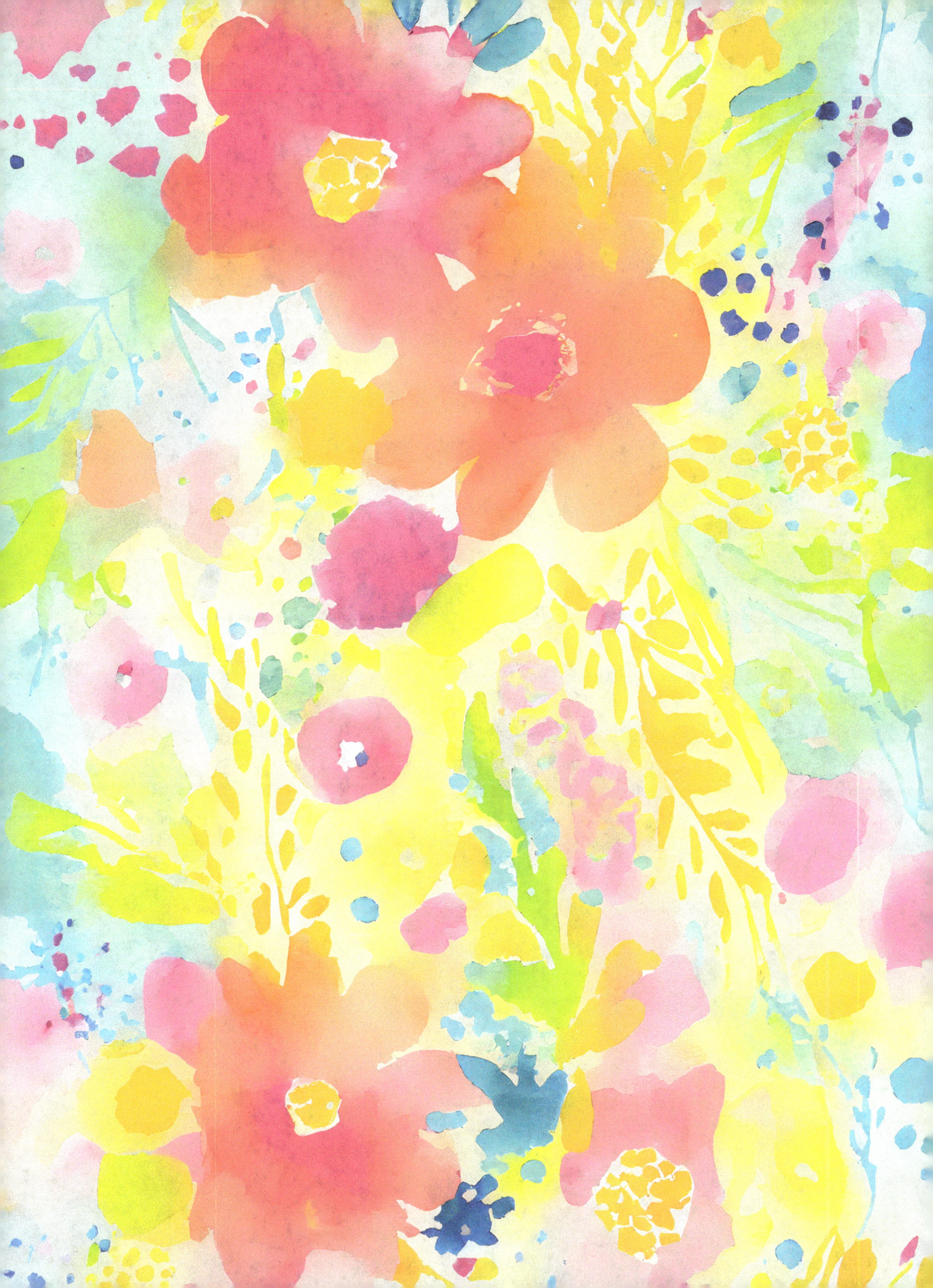

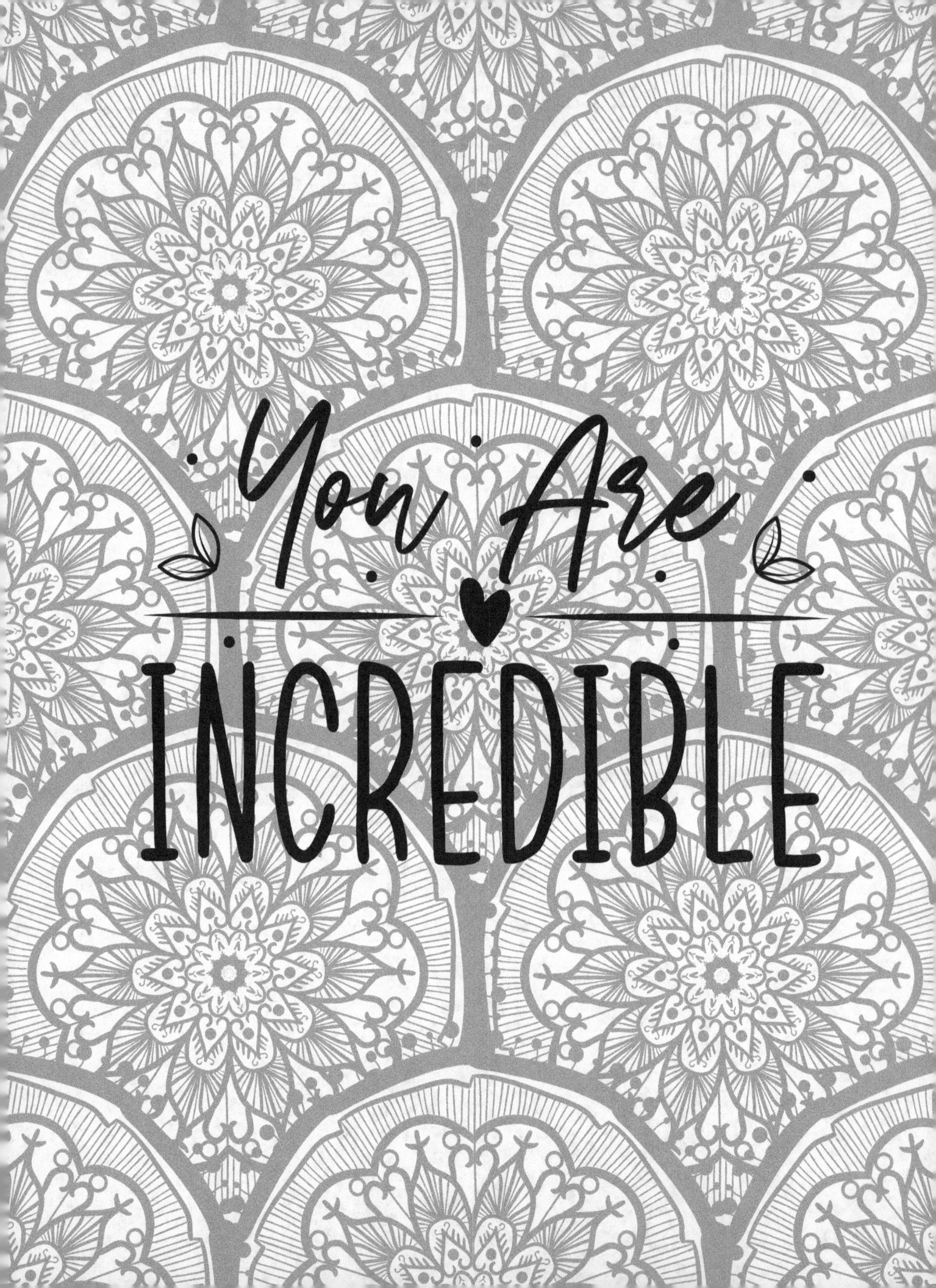

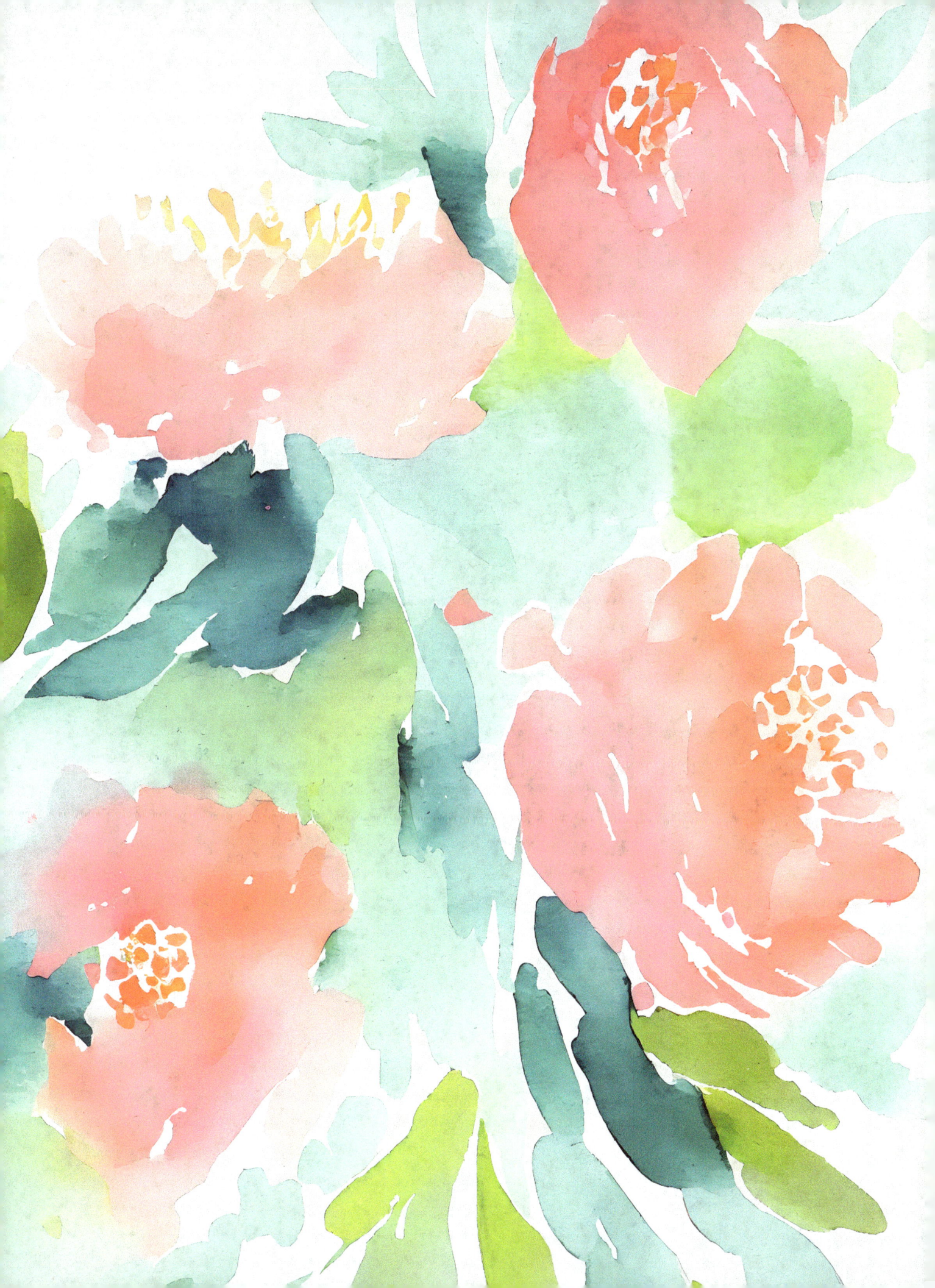

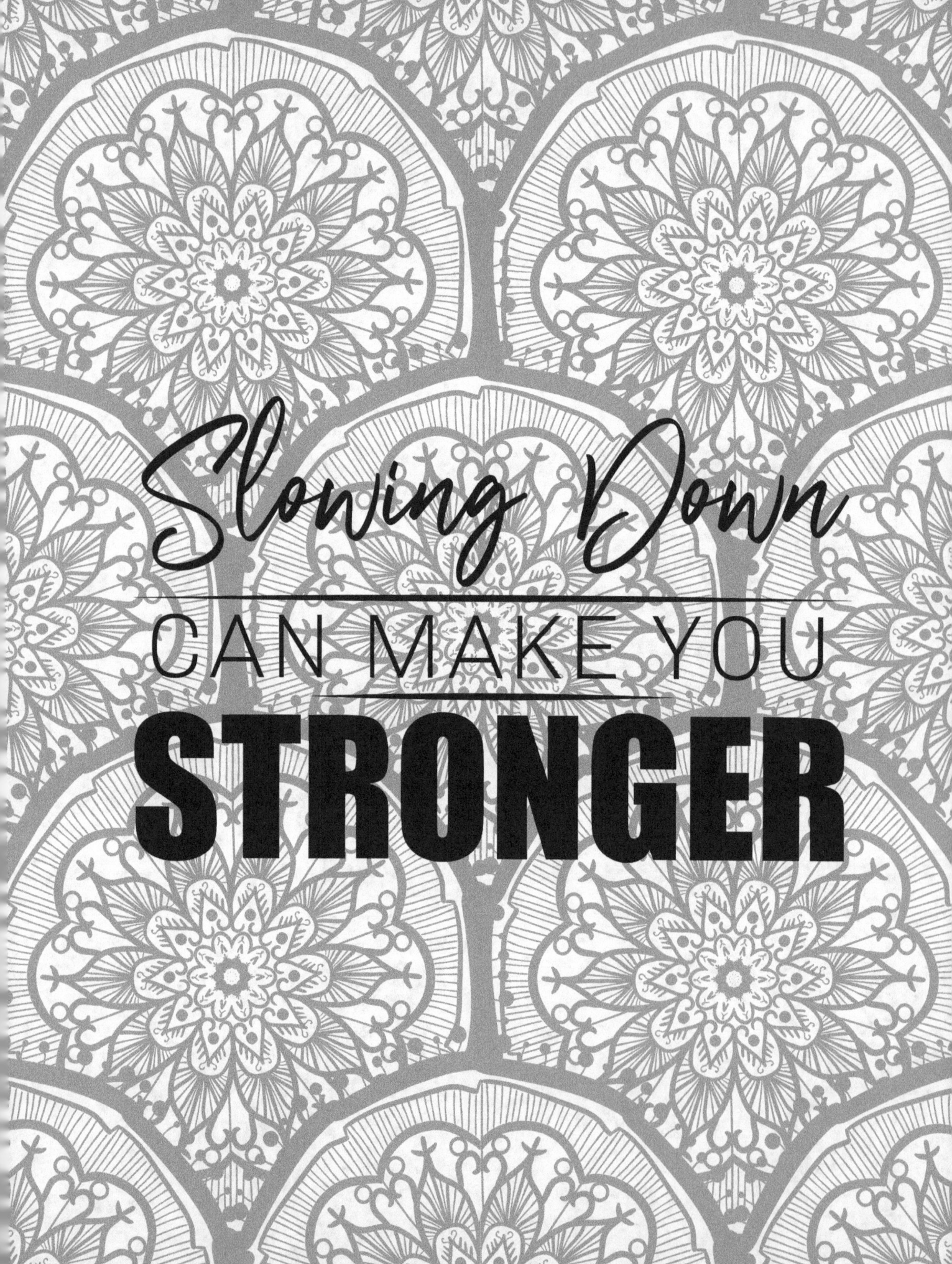

Slowing Down
CAN MAKE YOU
STRONGER

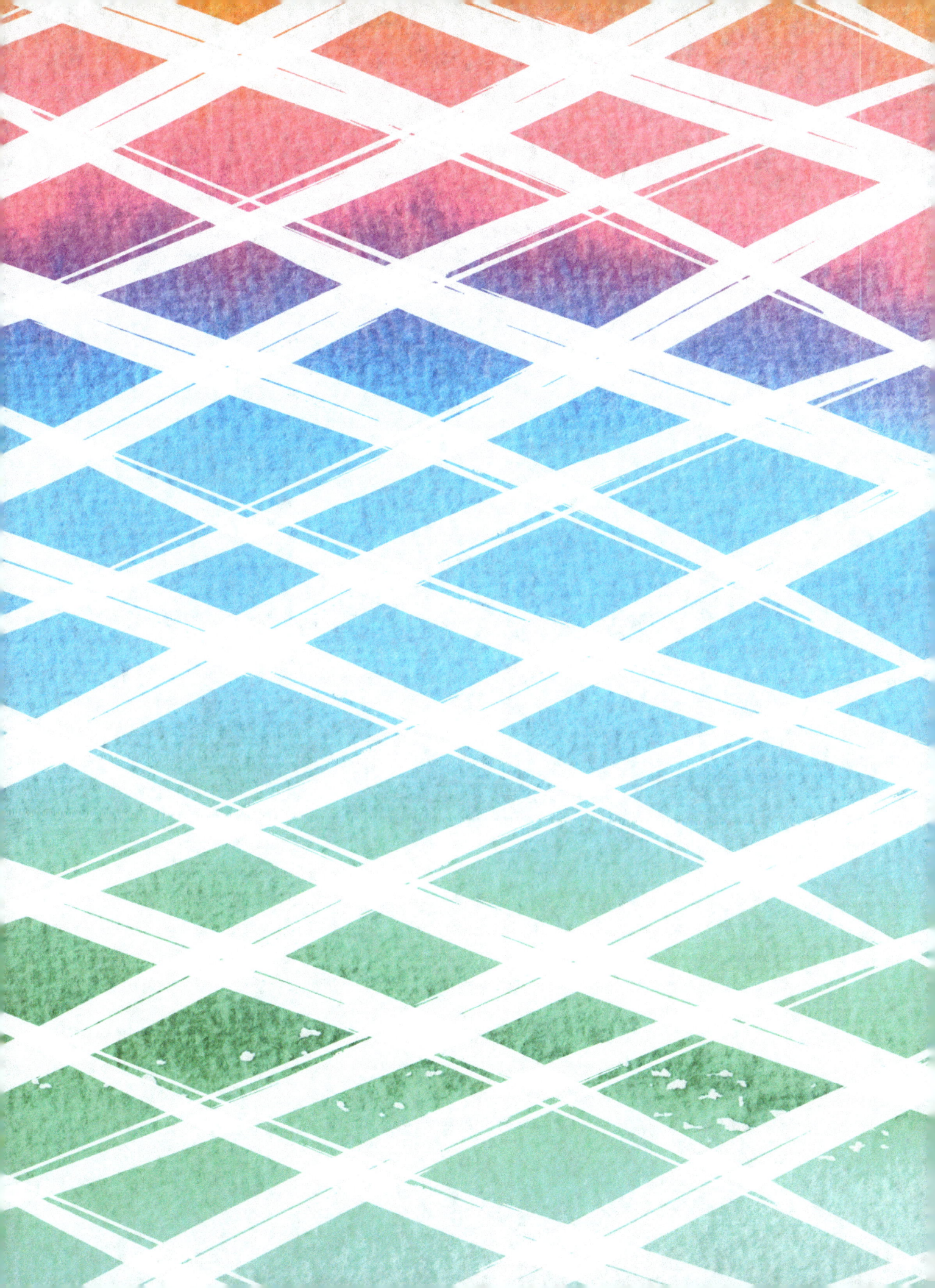

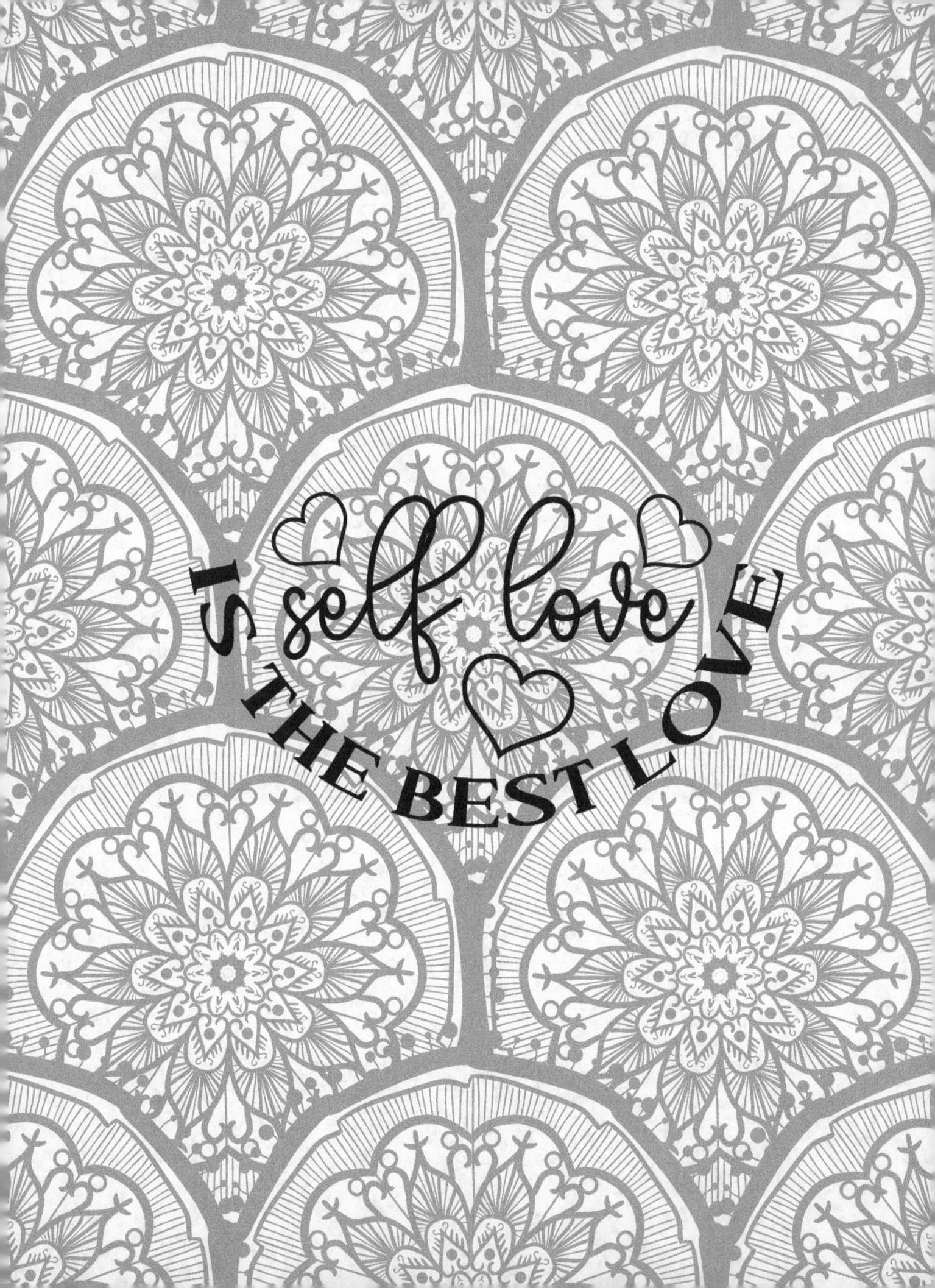

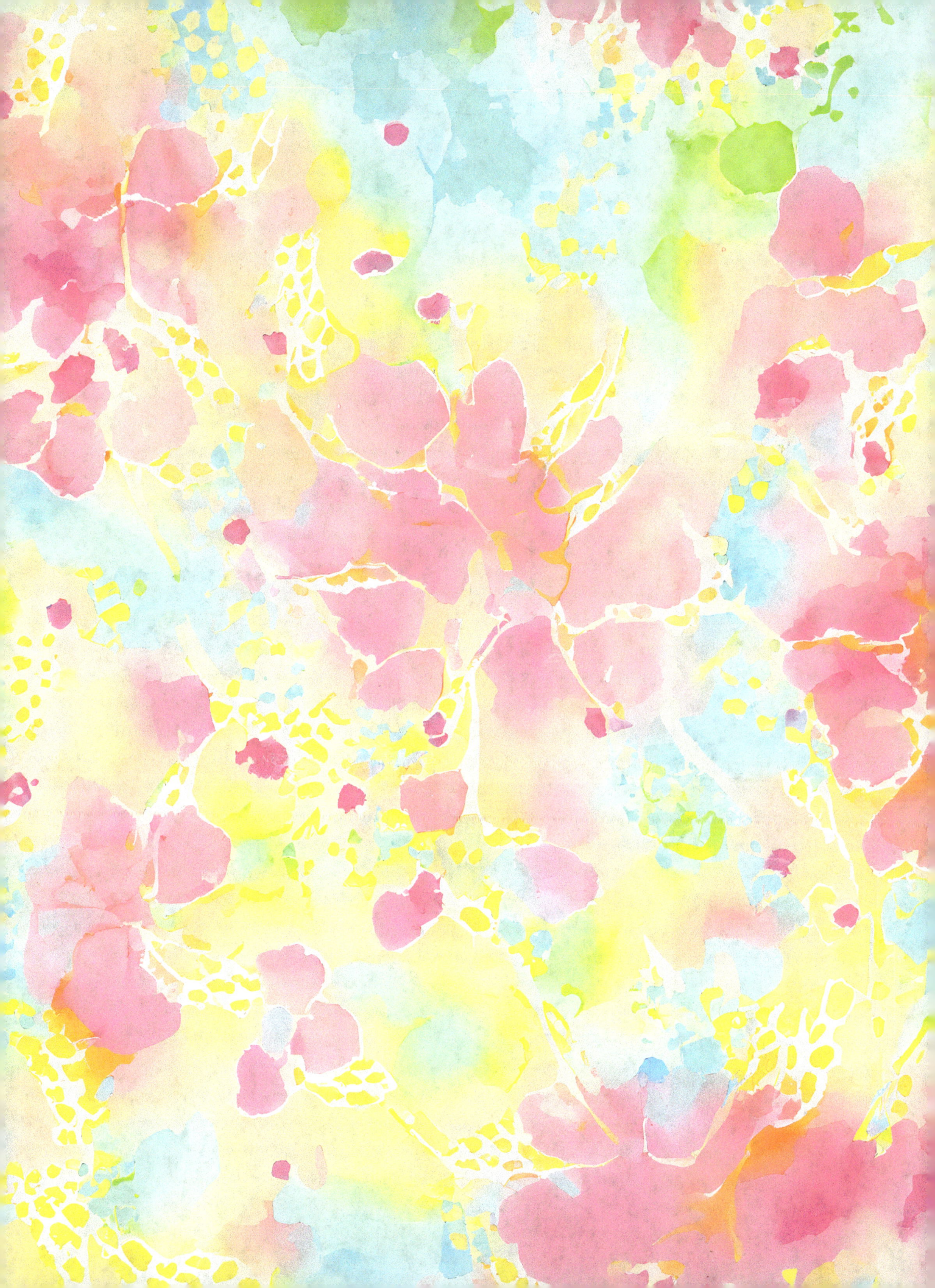

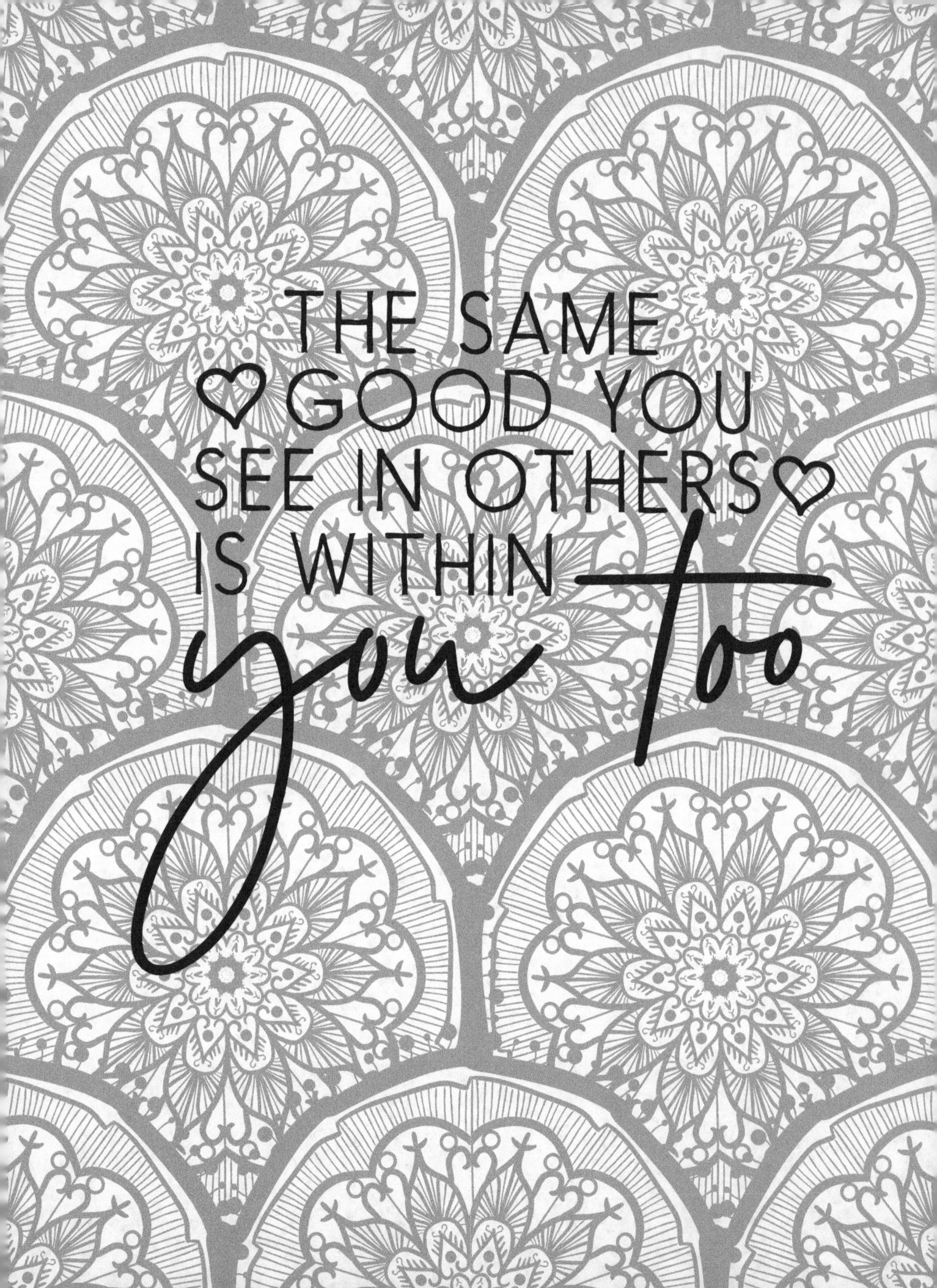

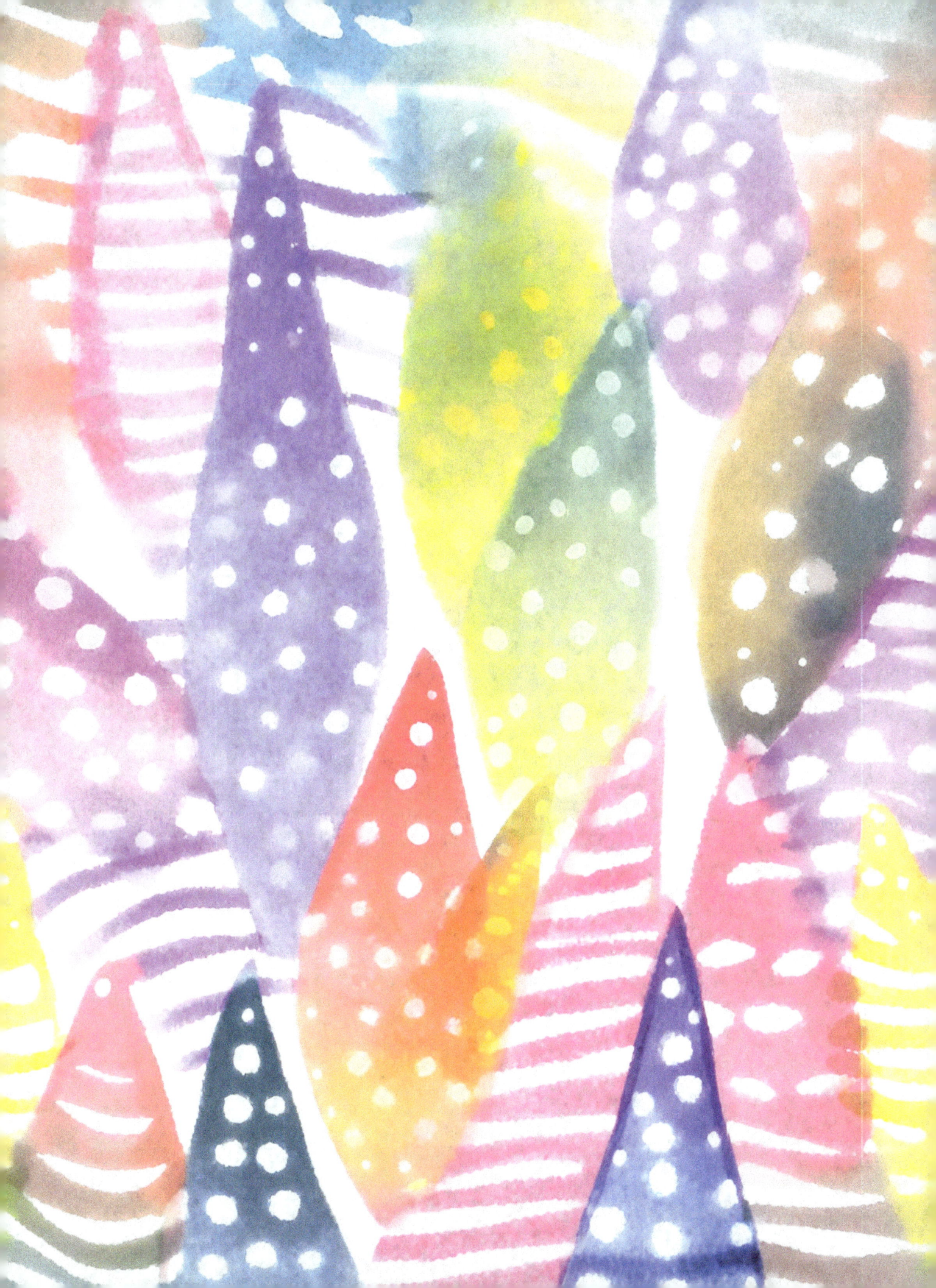

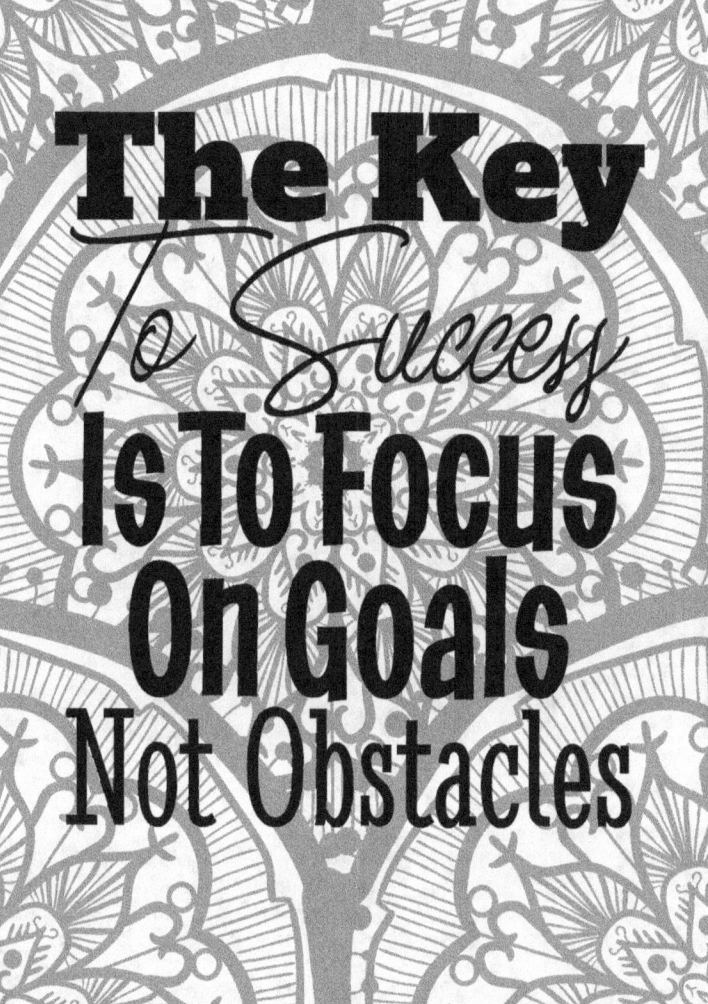

The Key To Success Is To Focus On Goals Not Obstacles

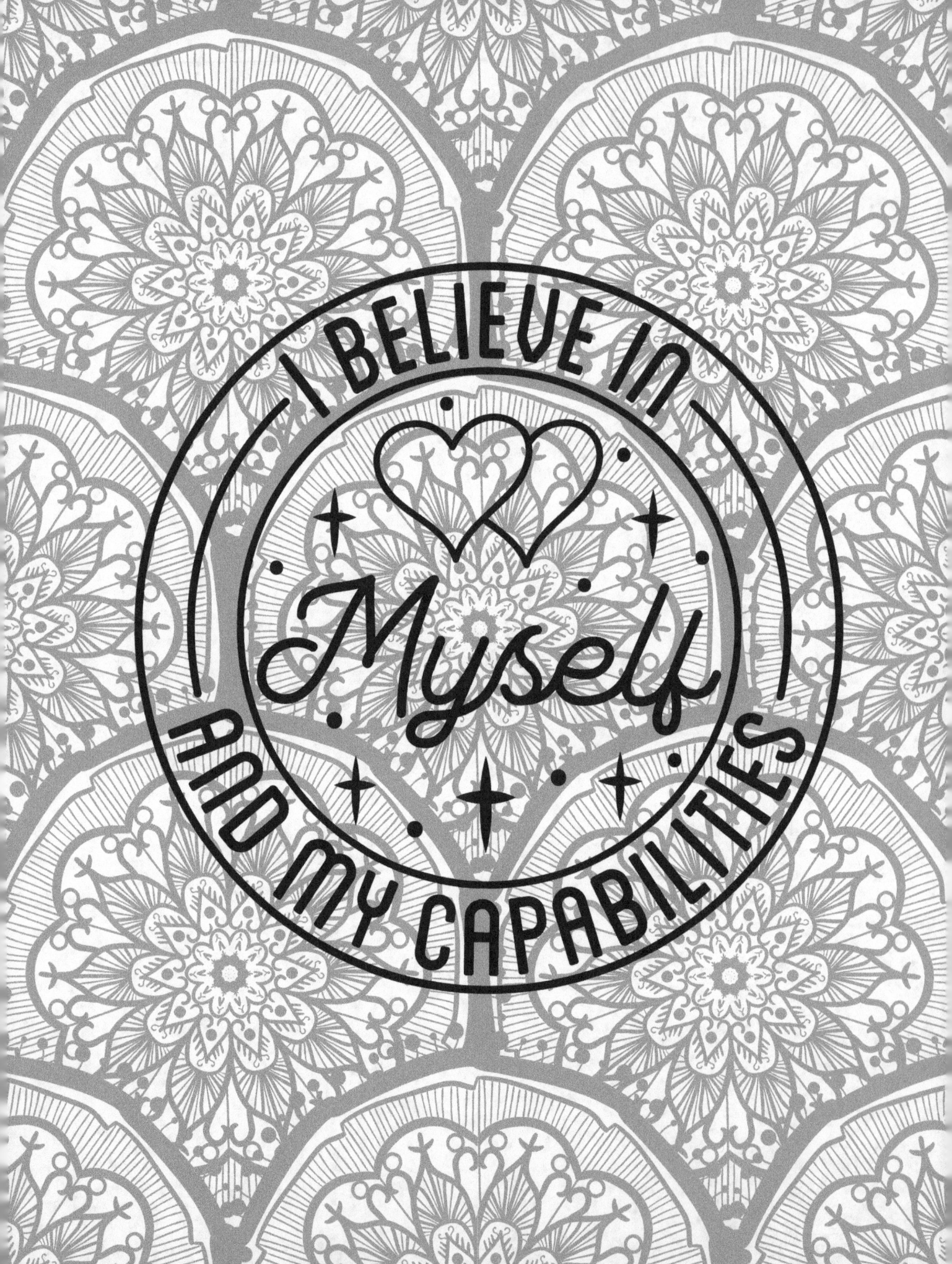

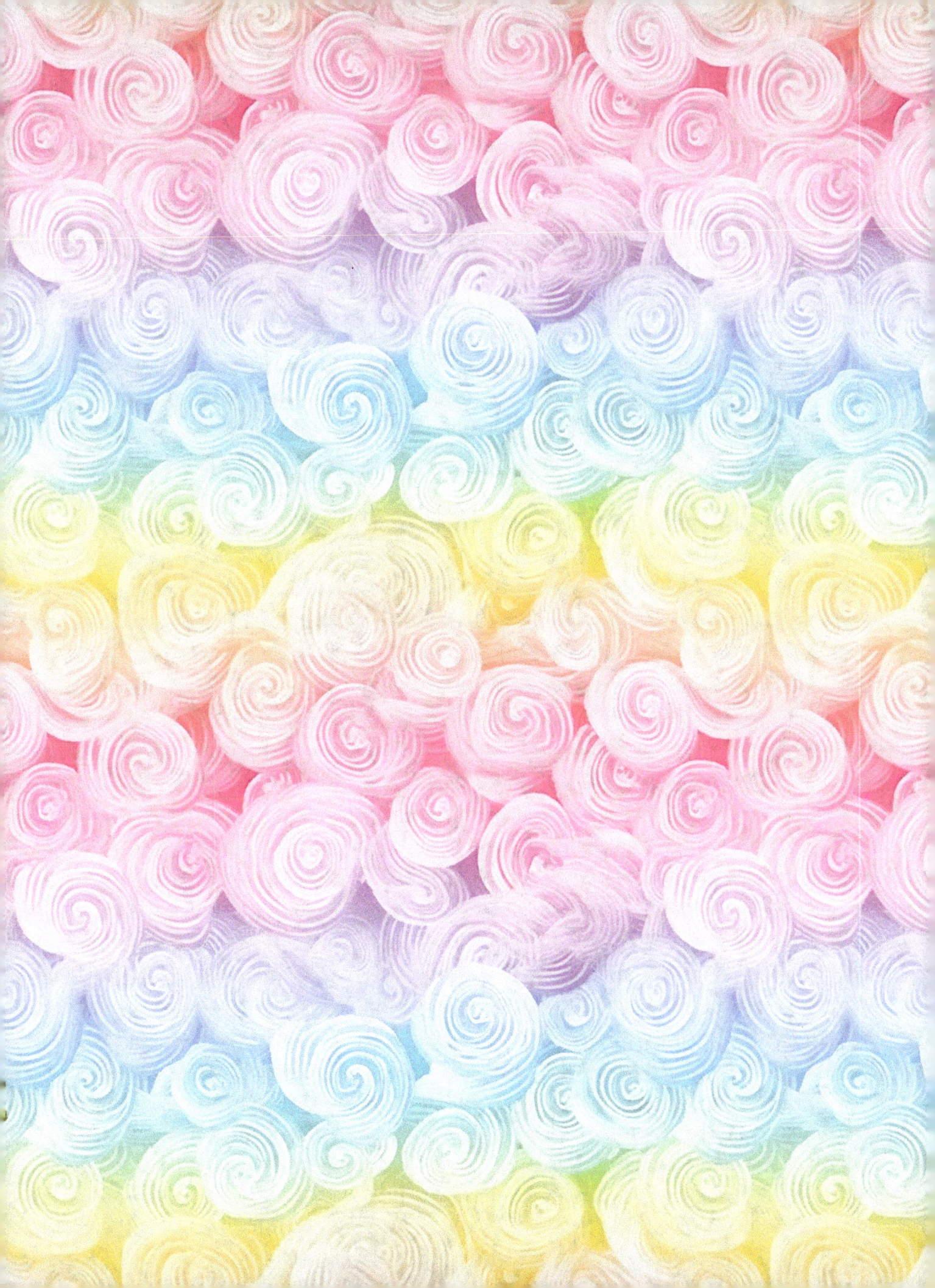

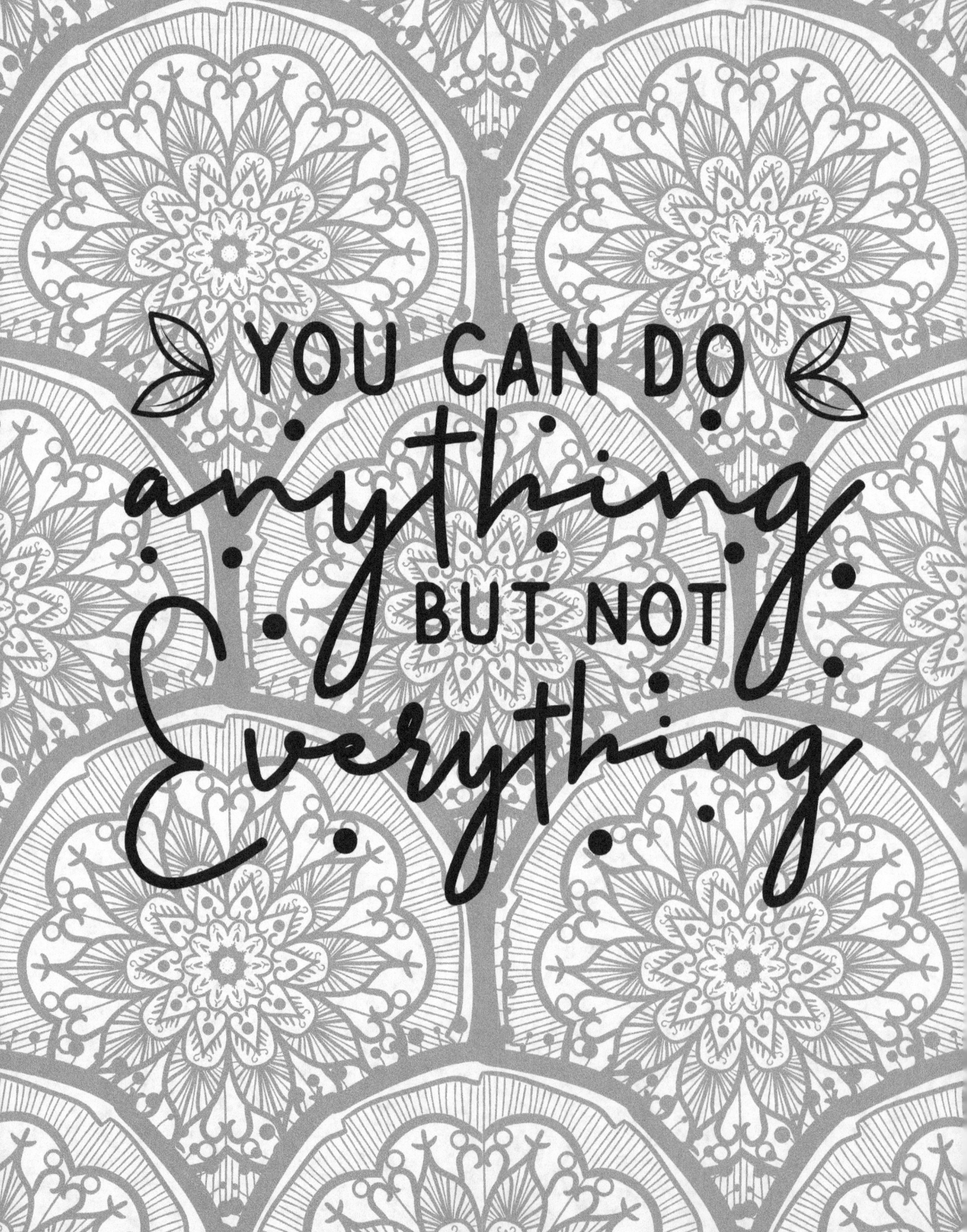

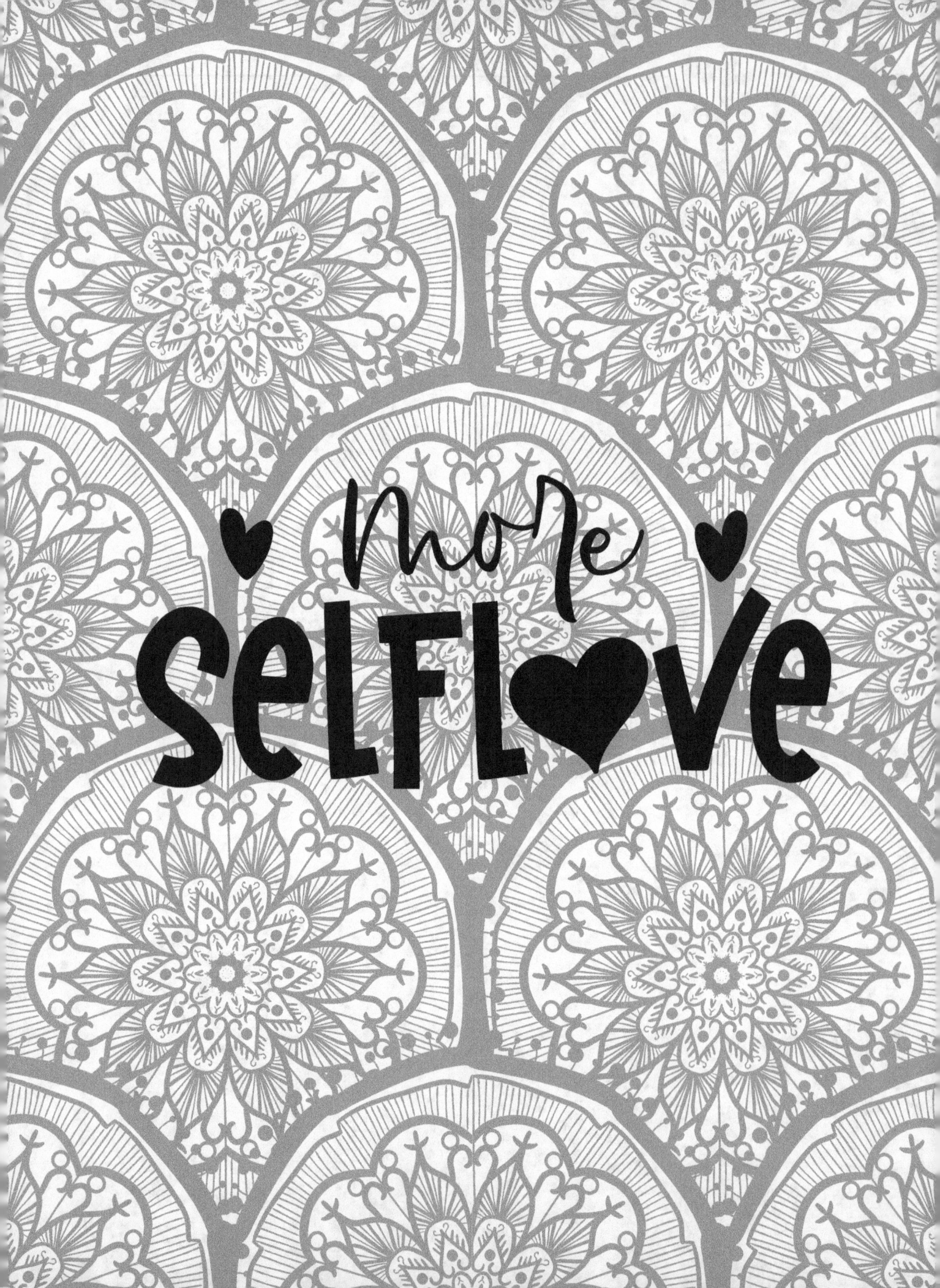

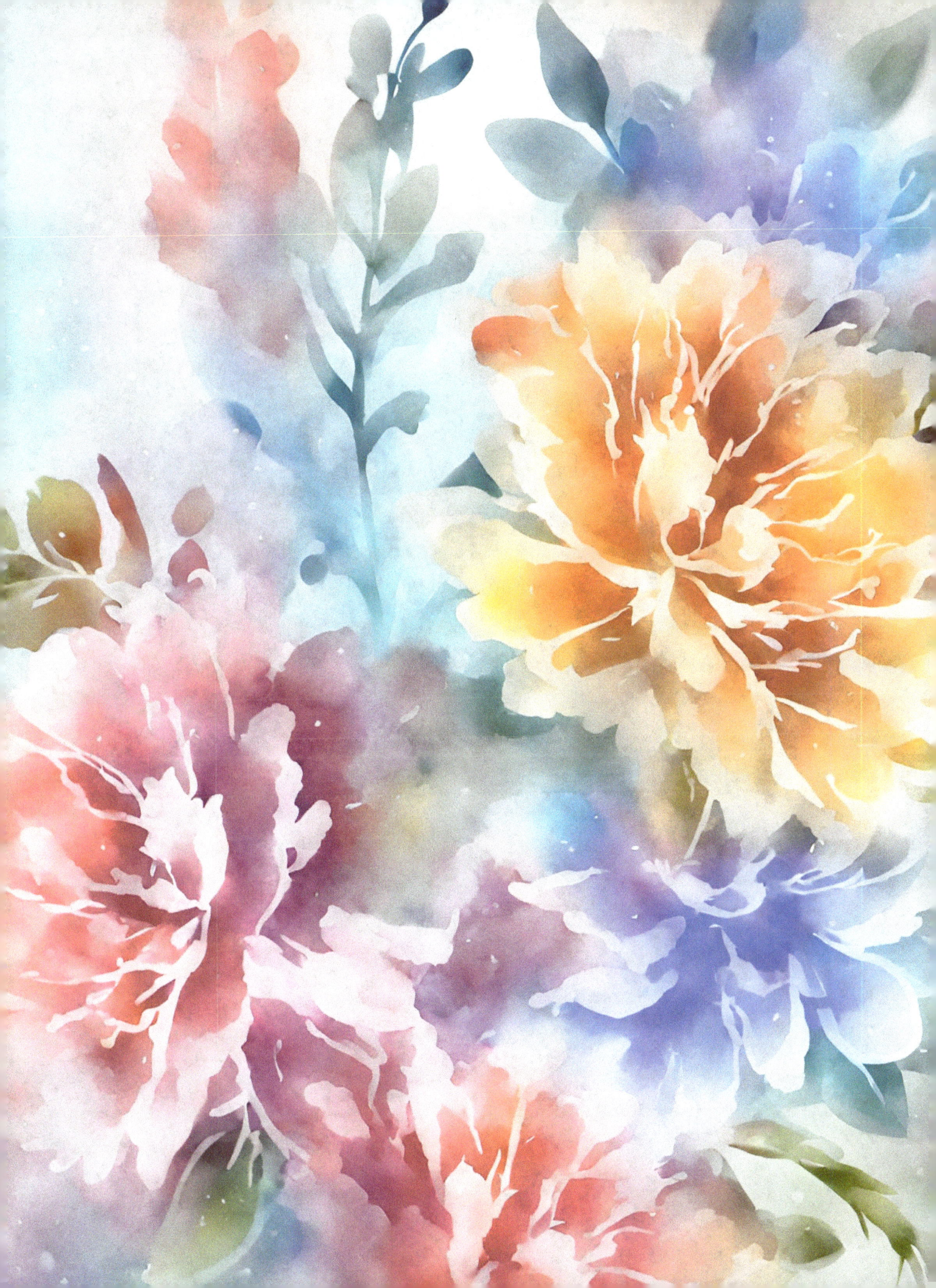

BE YOUR OWN TYPE OF

Perfect

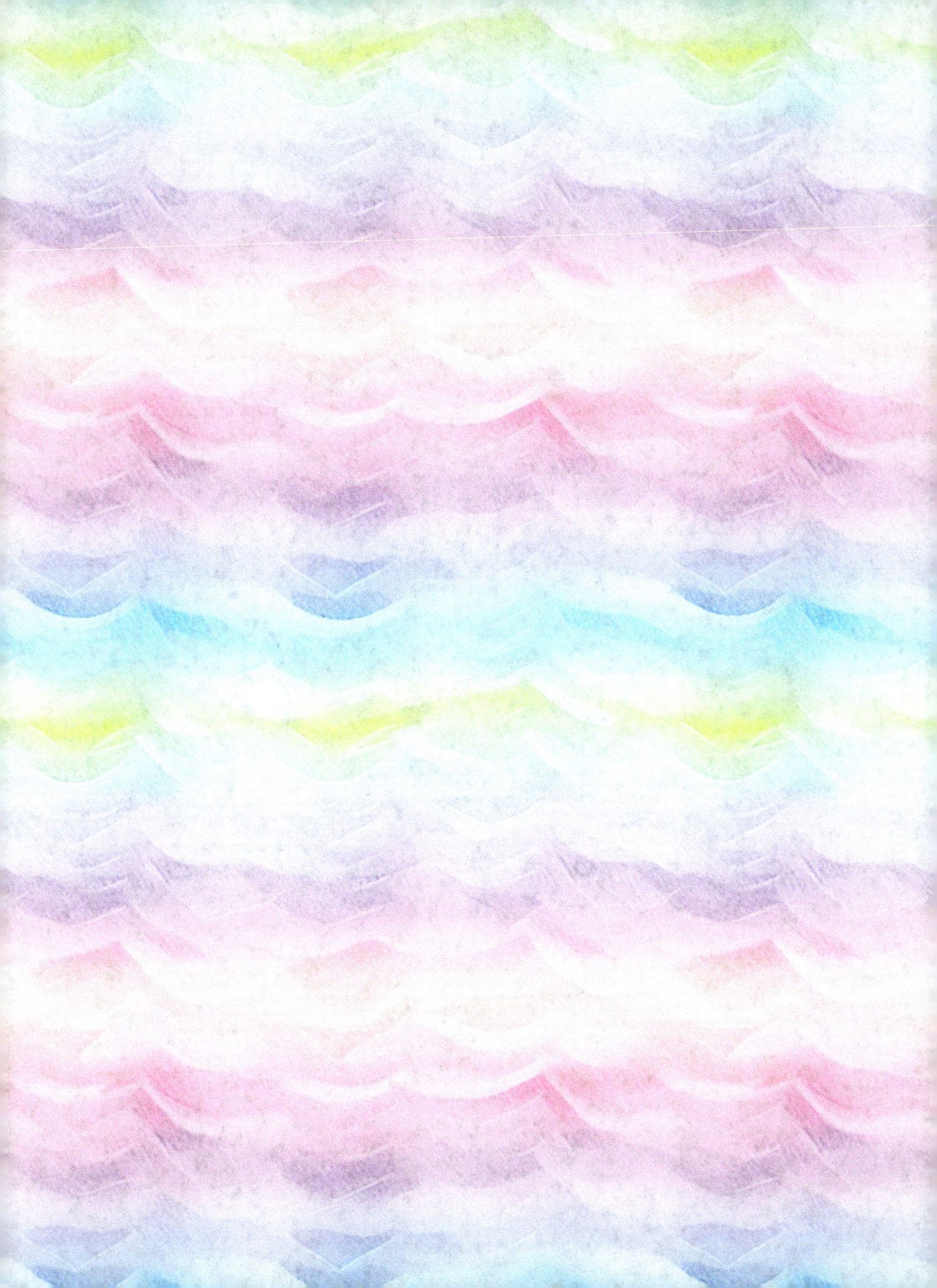

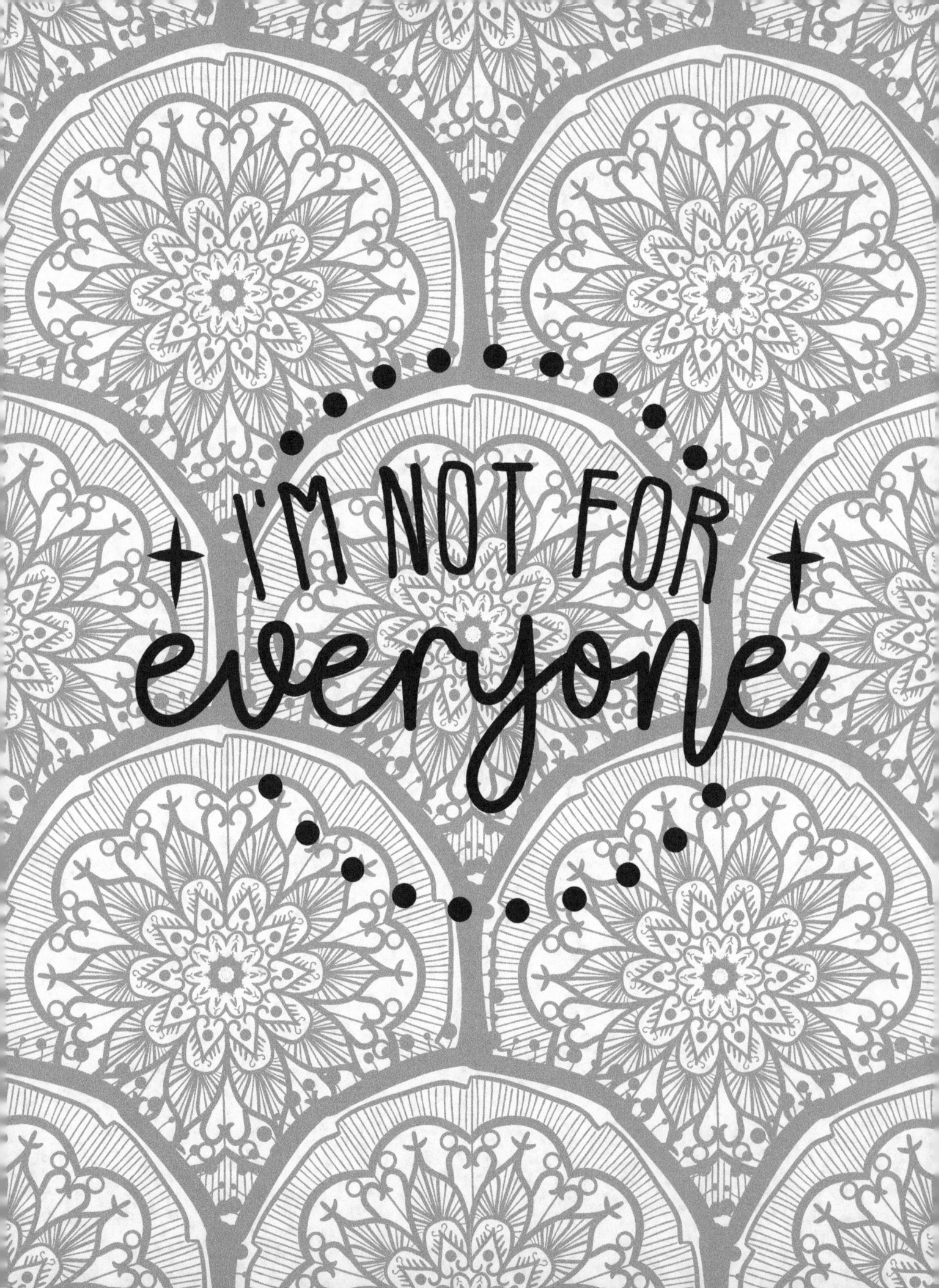

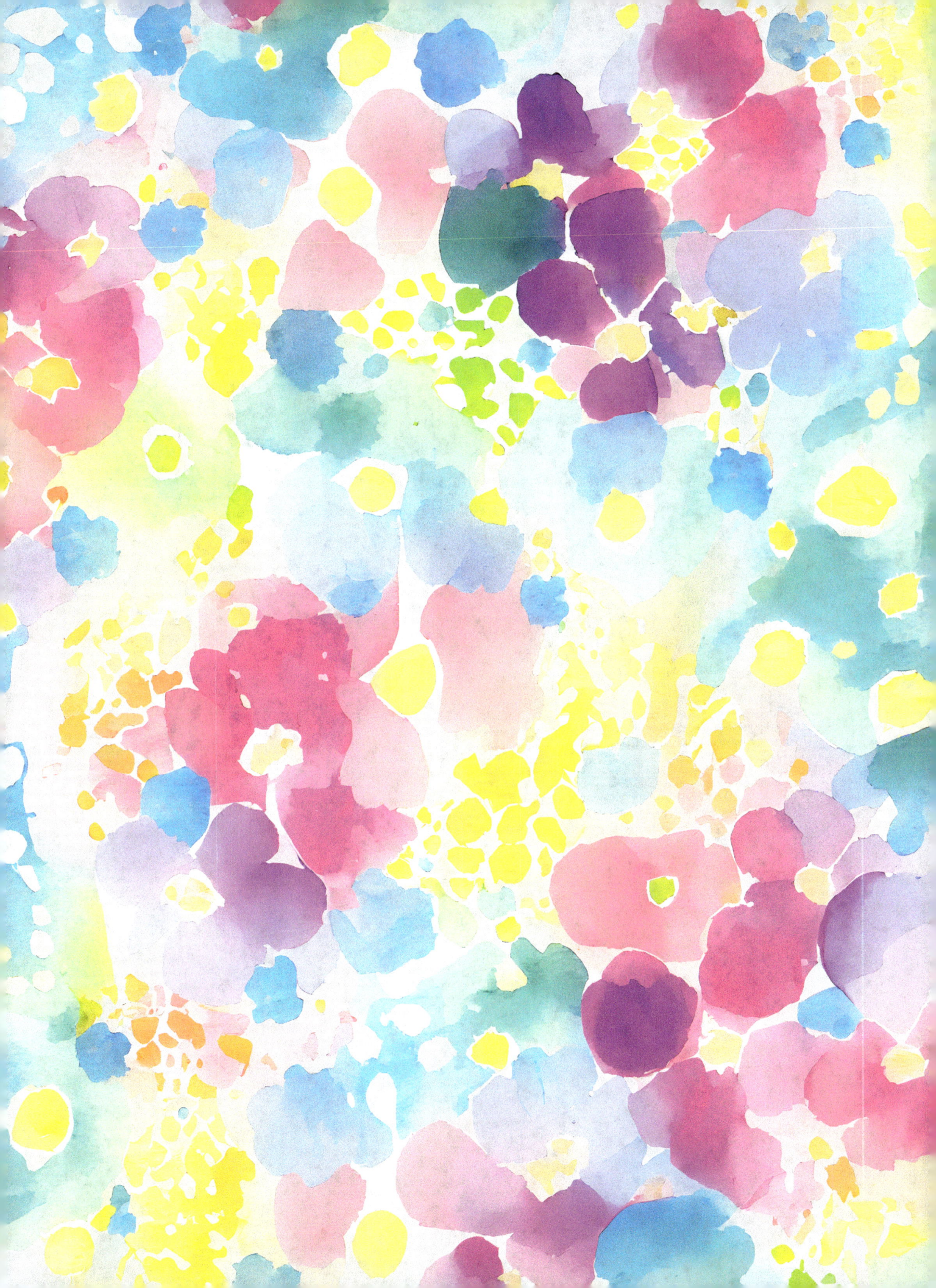

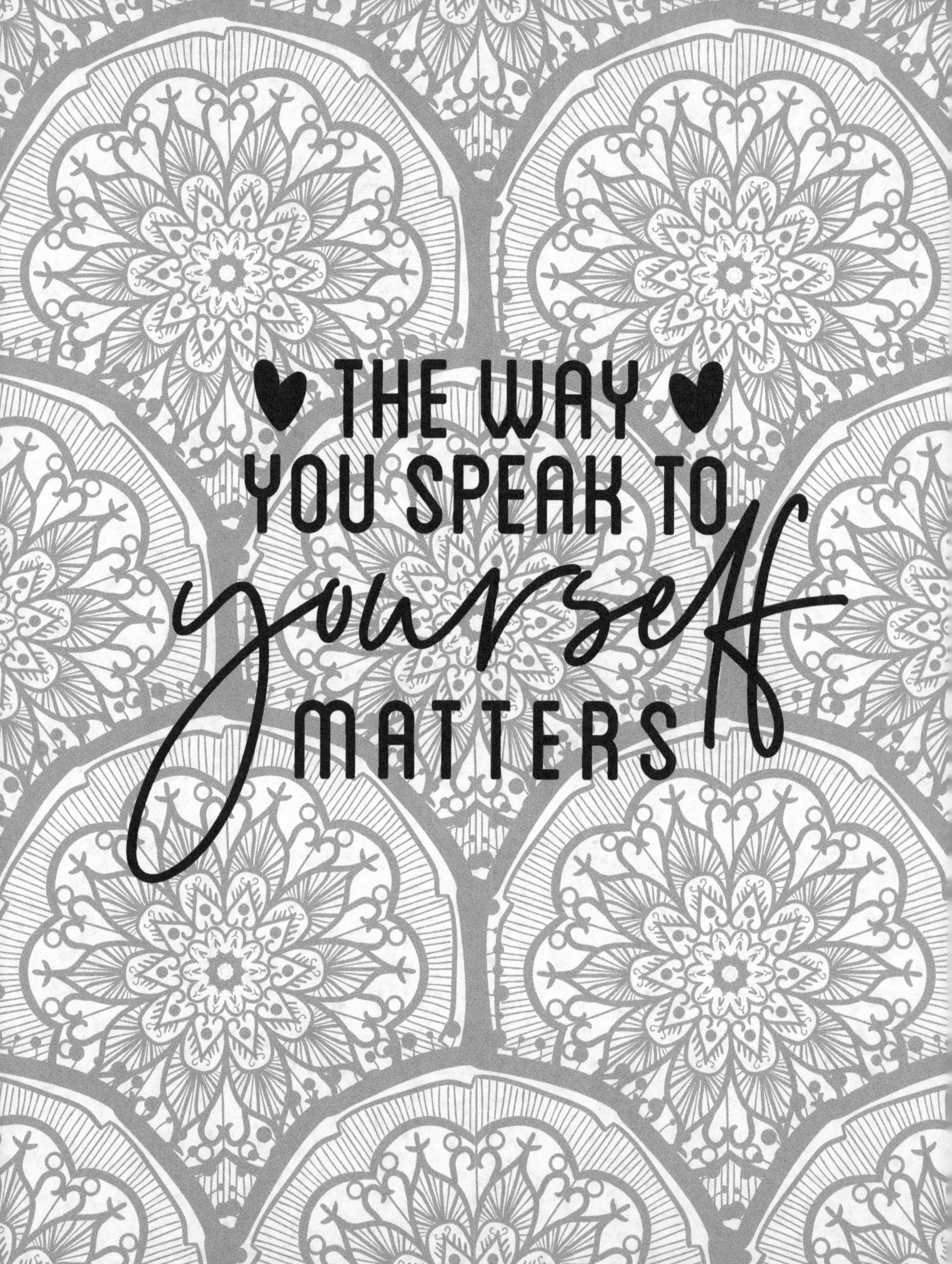

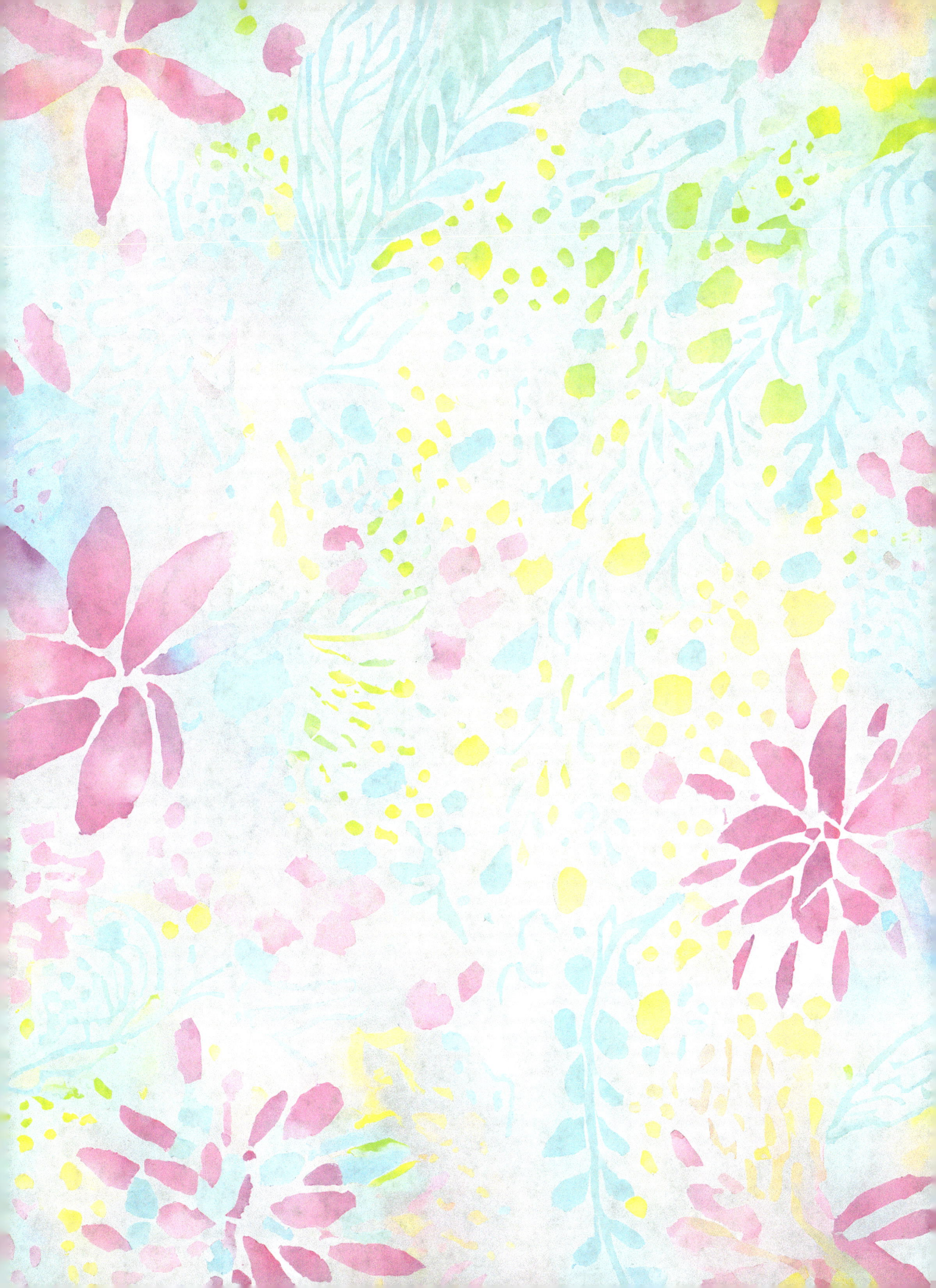

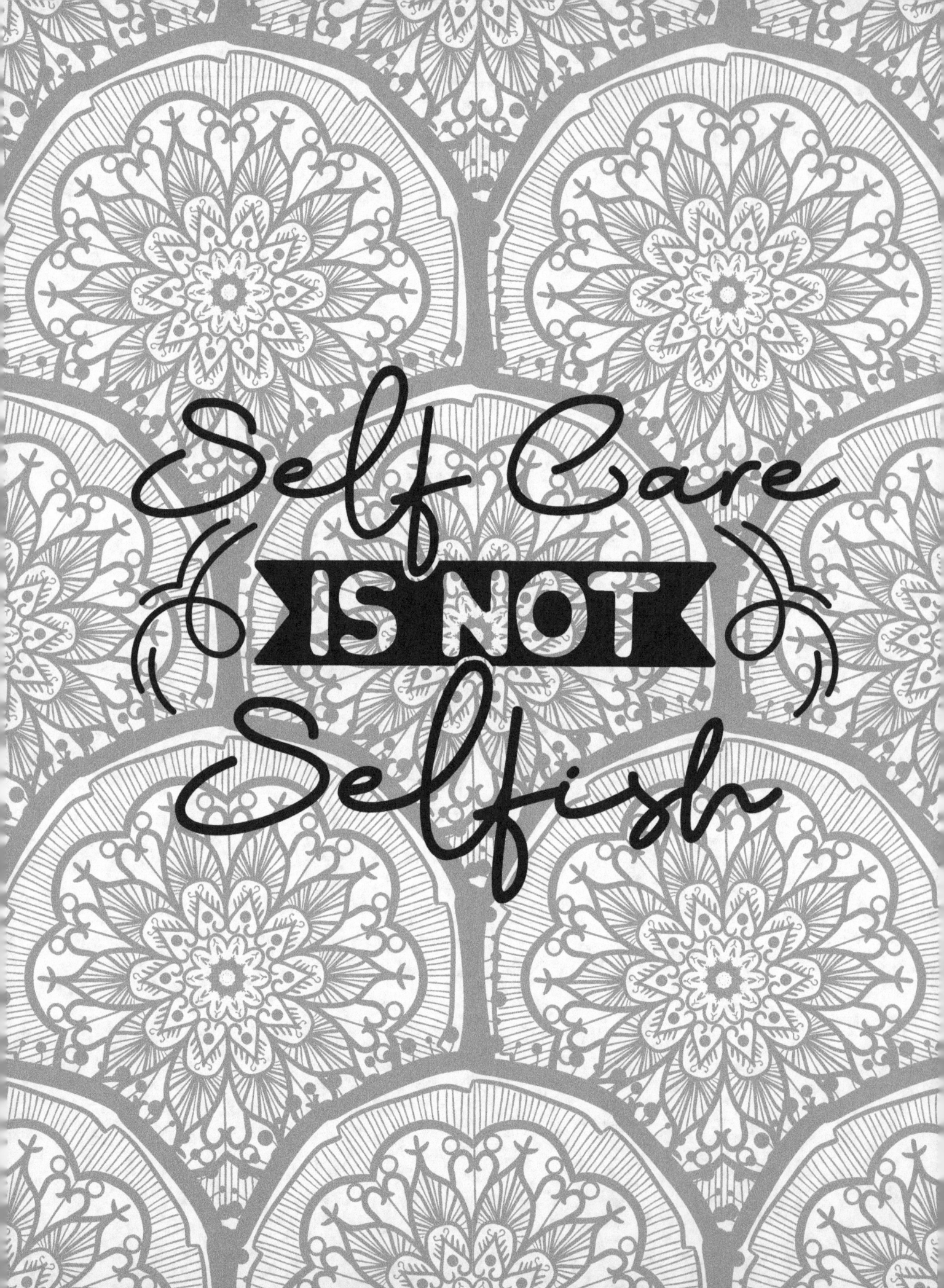

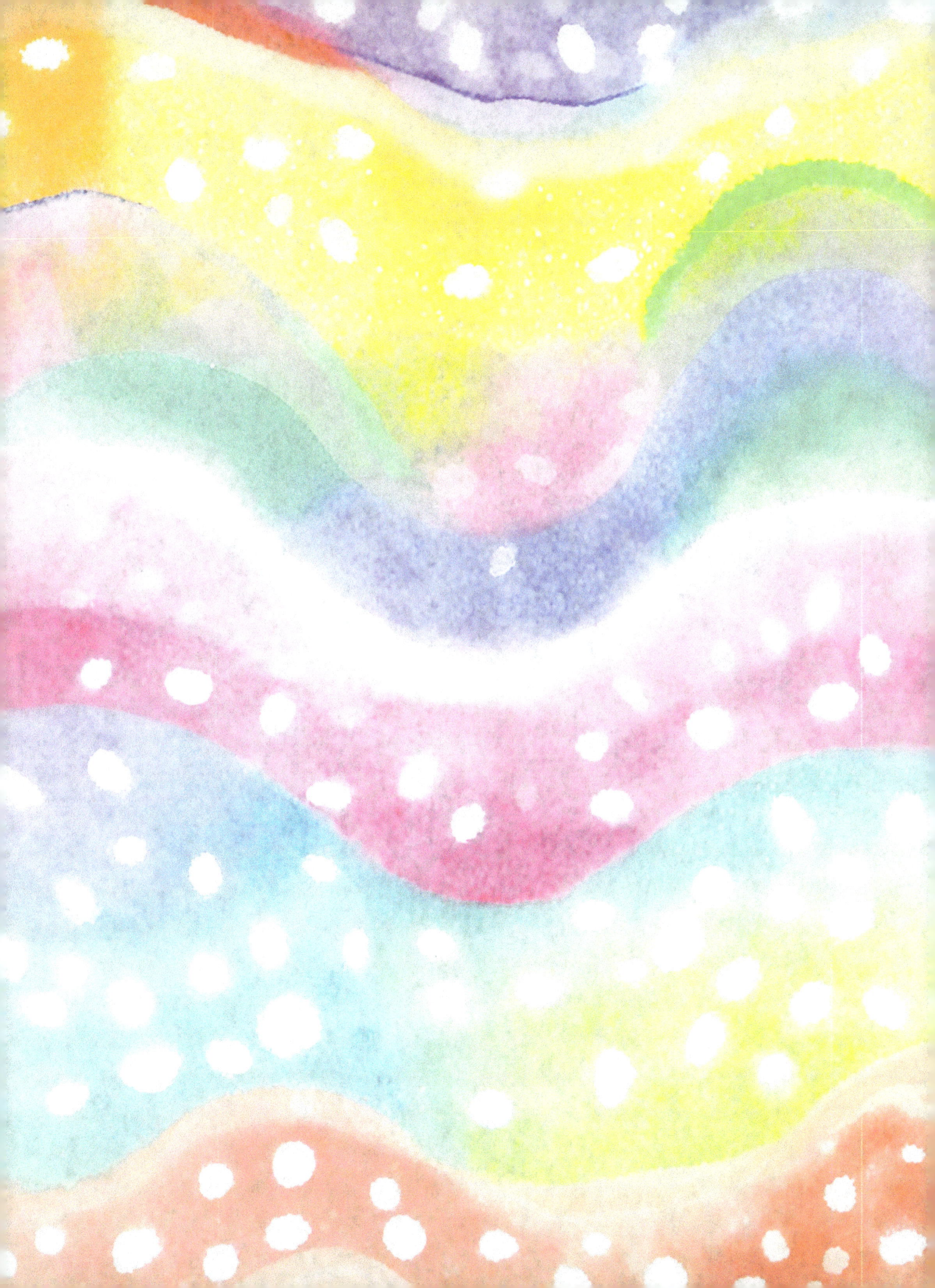

Embrace

THE GLORIOUS MESS
• THAT YOU ARE •

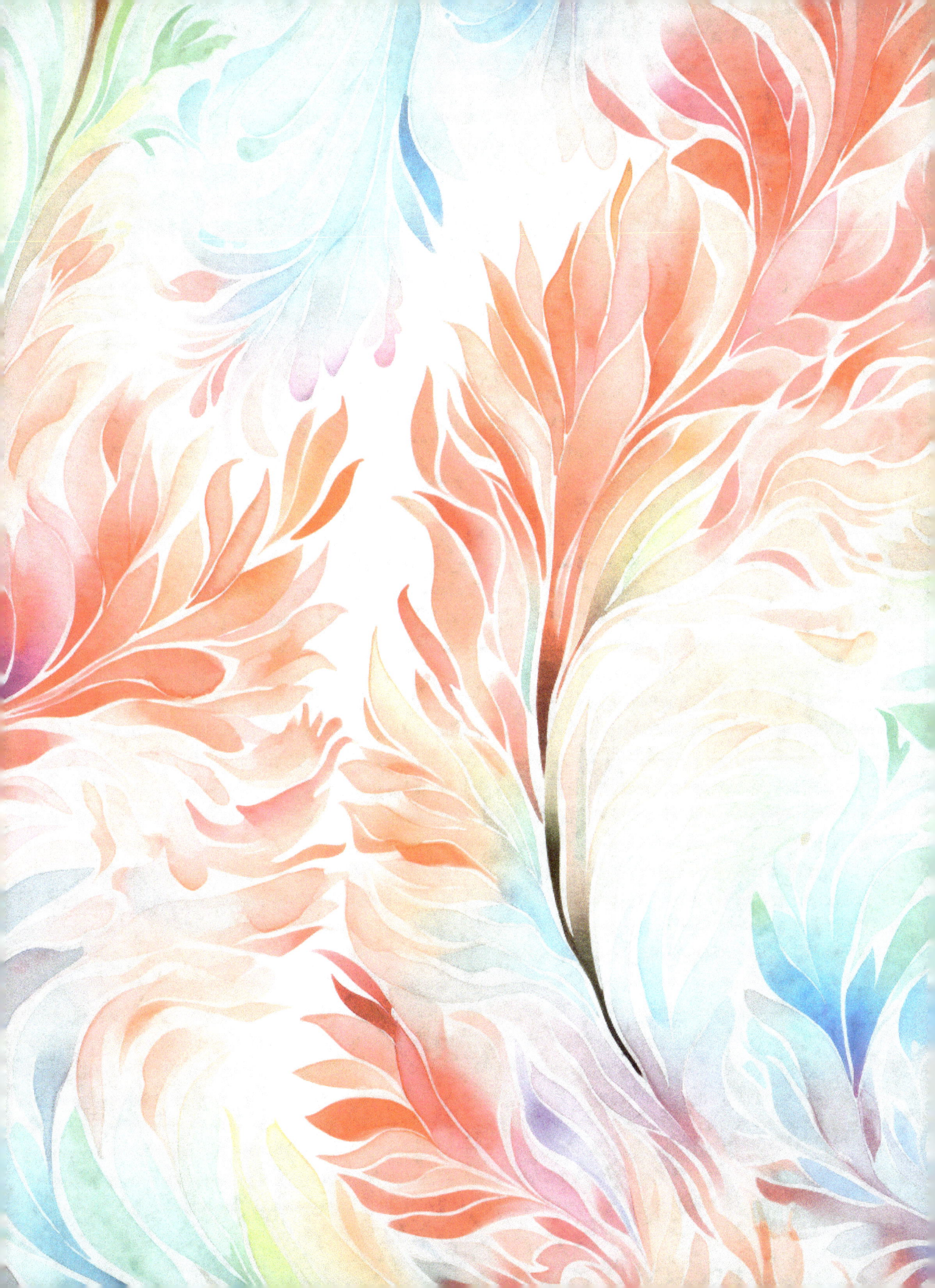

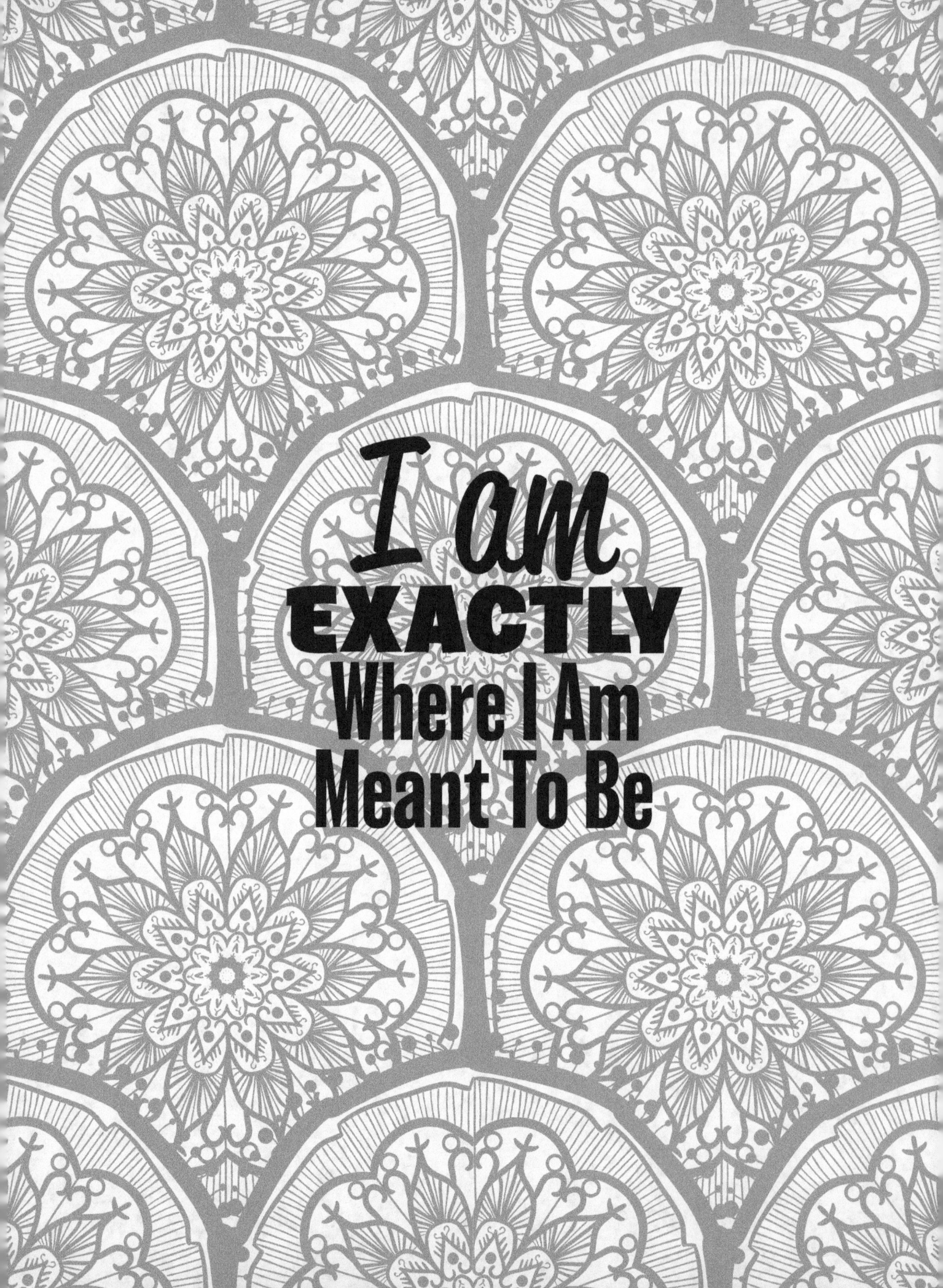

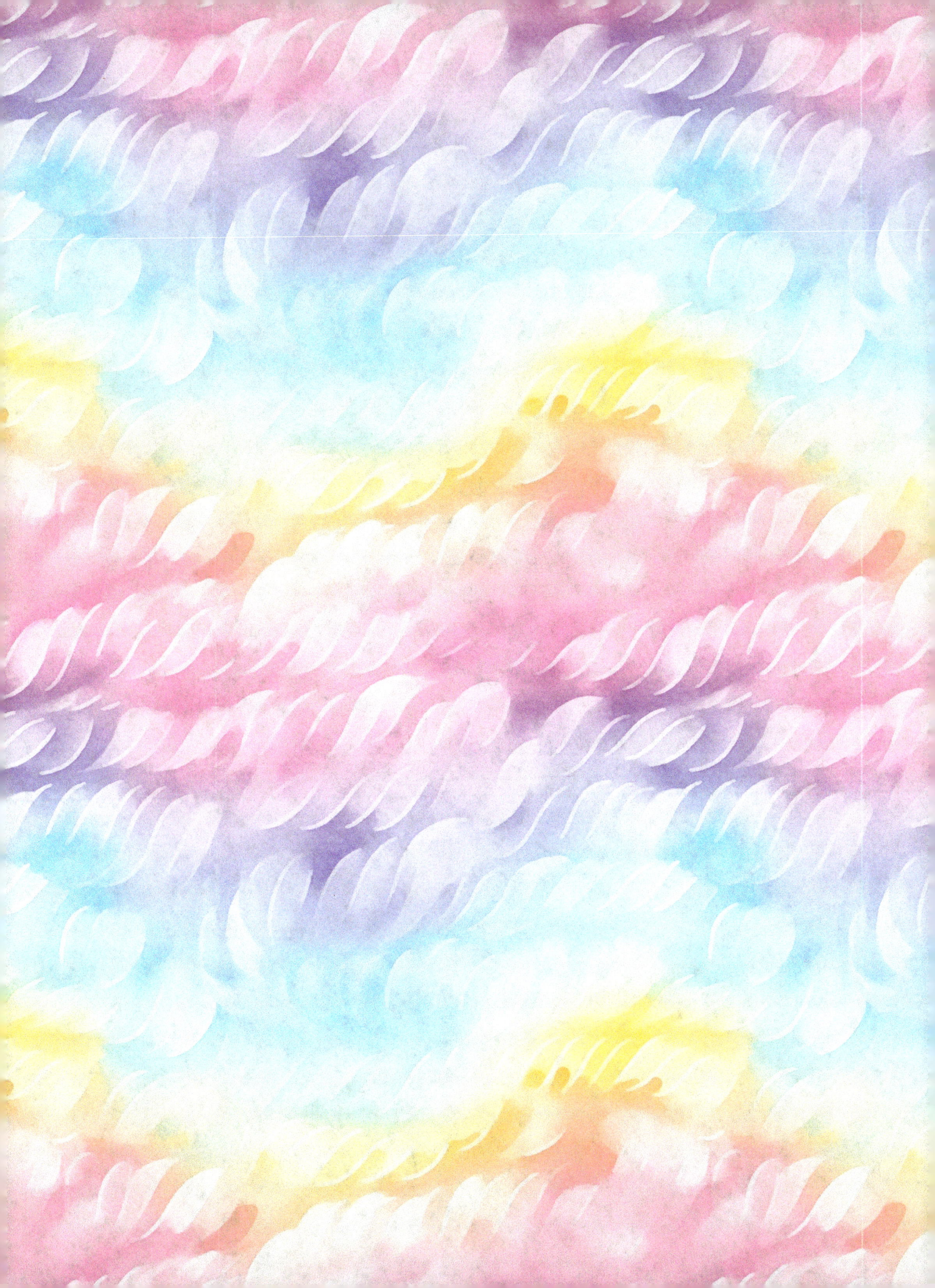

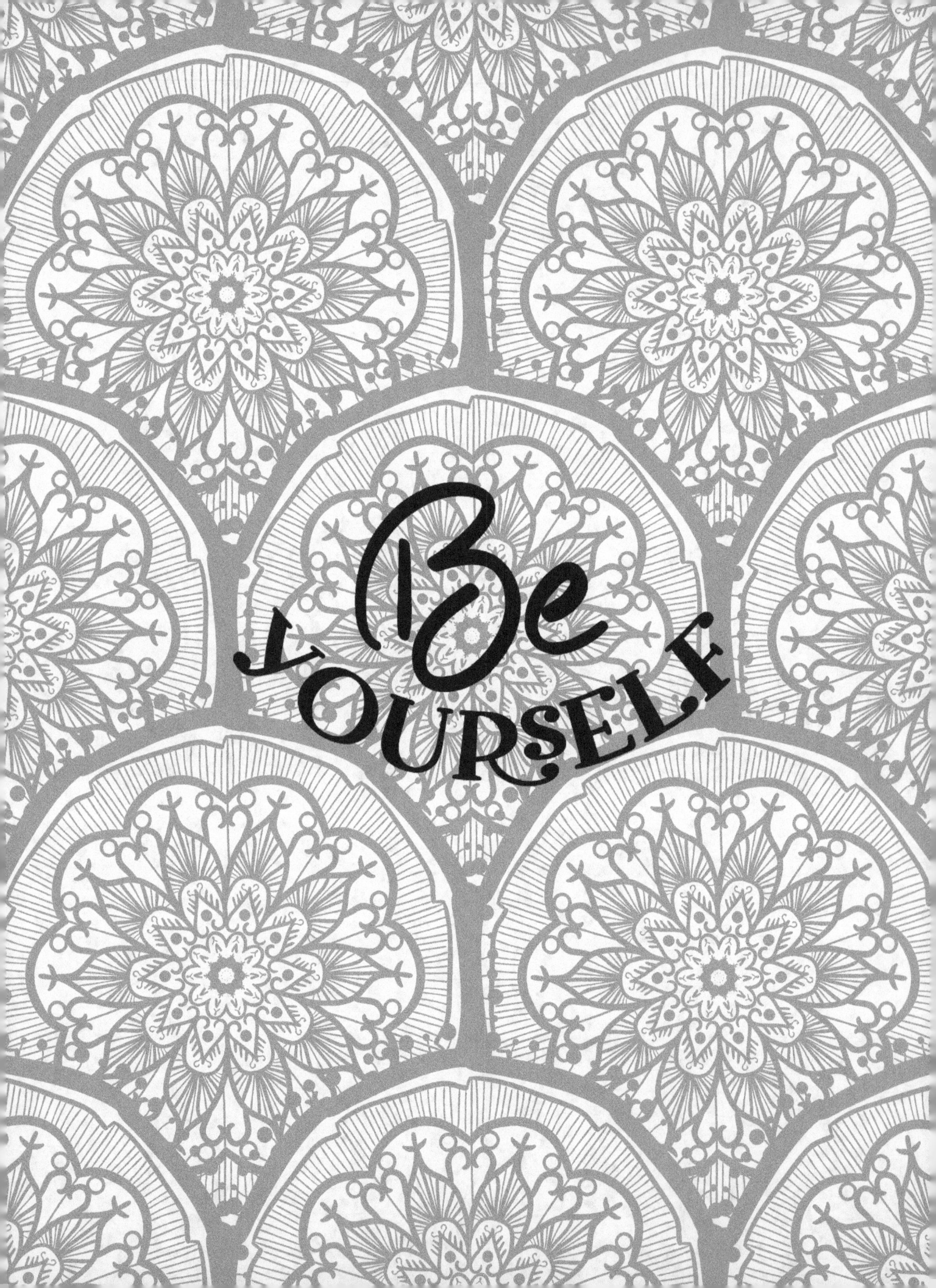

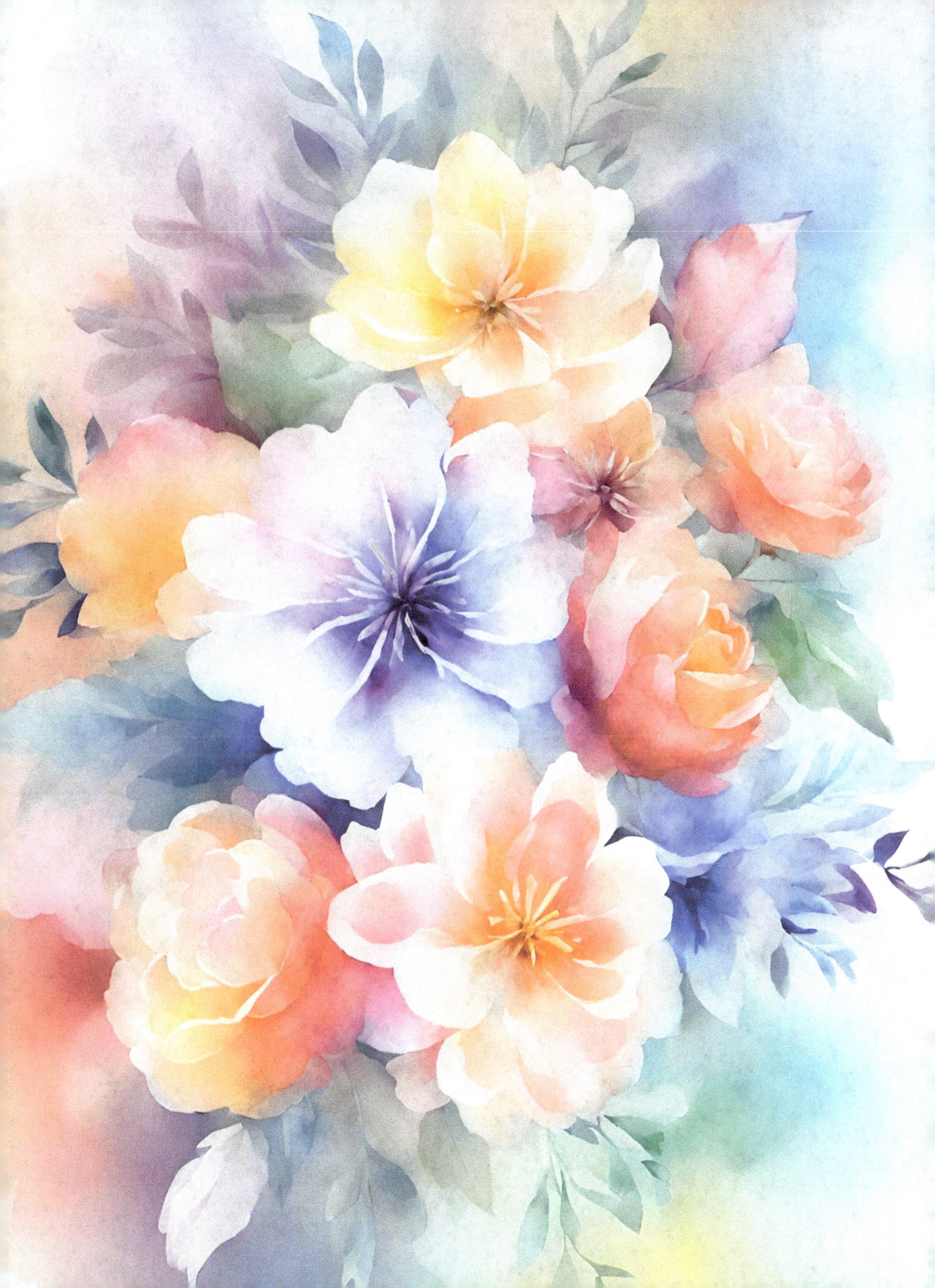

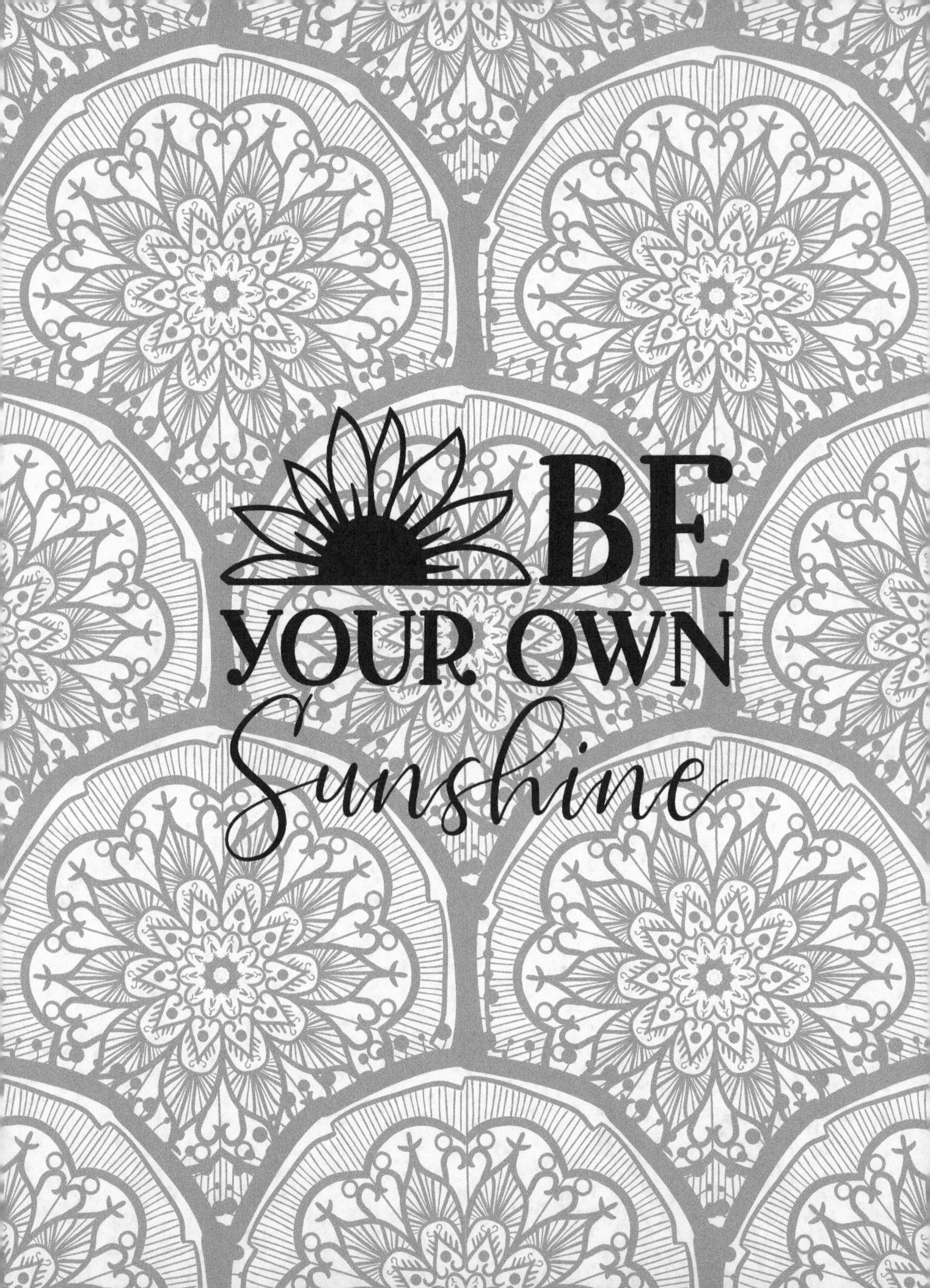

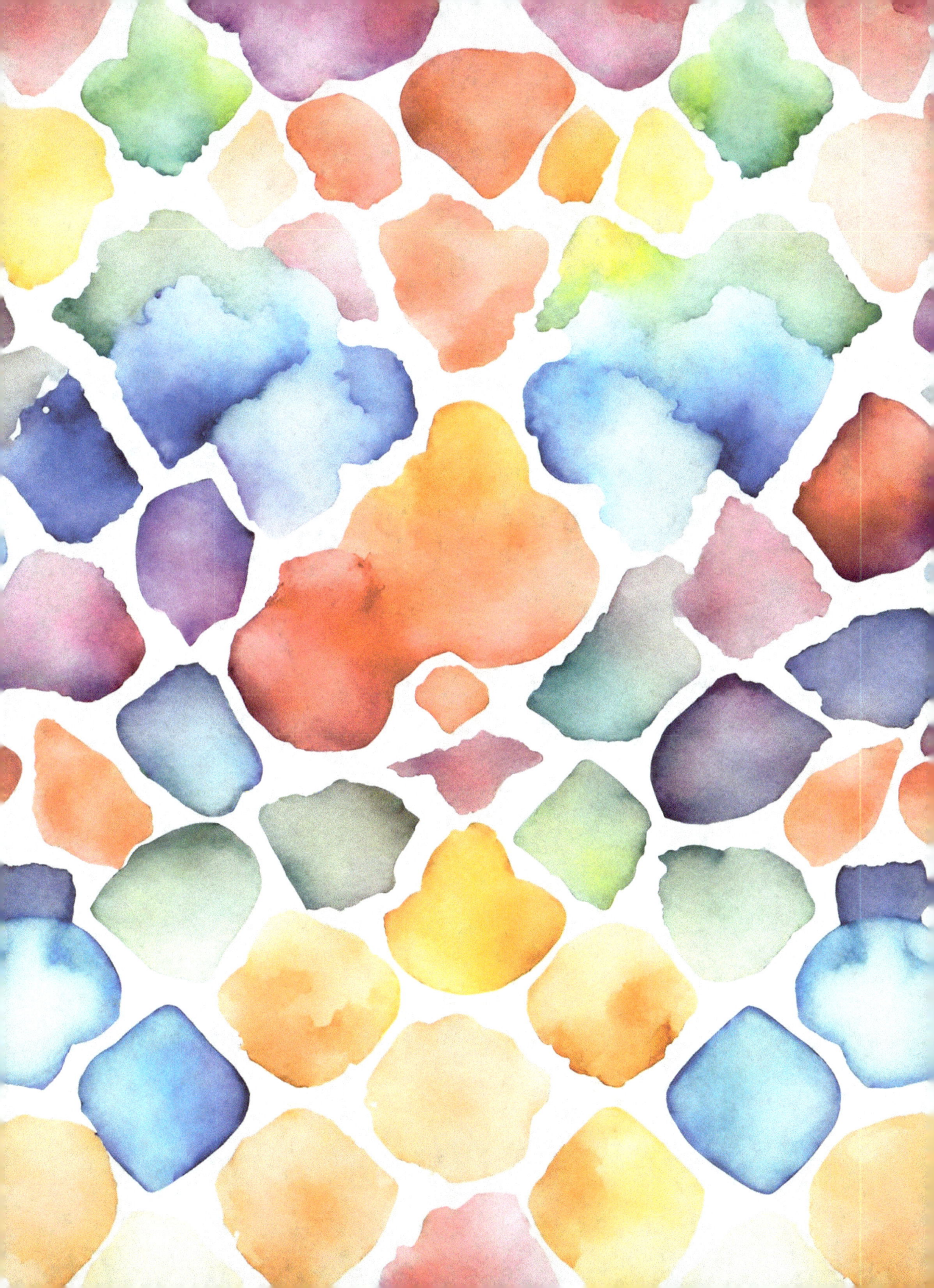

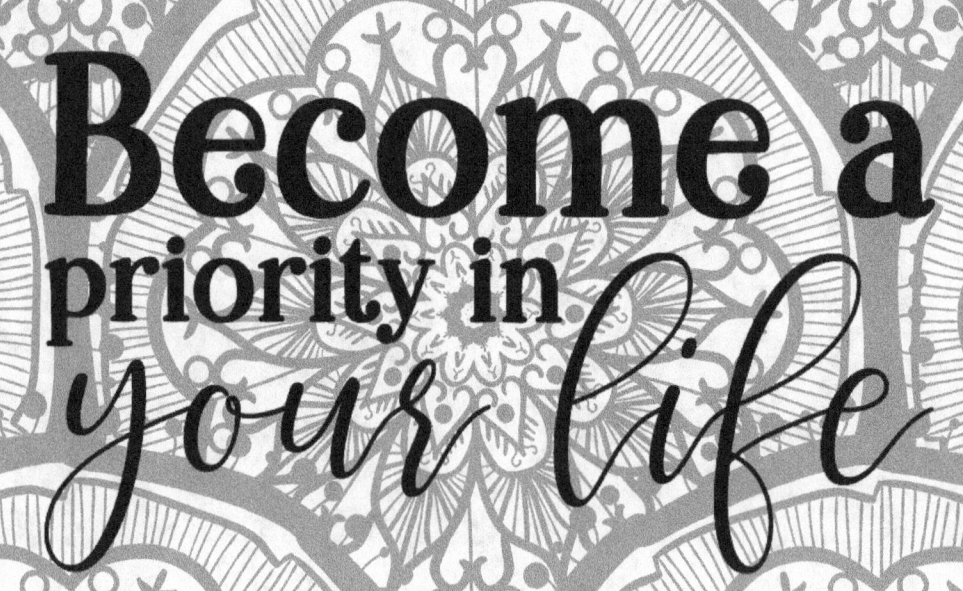

Become a
priority in
your life

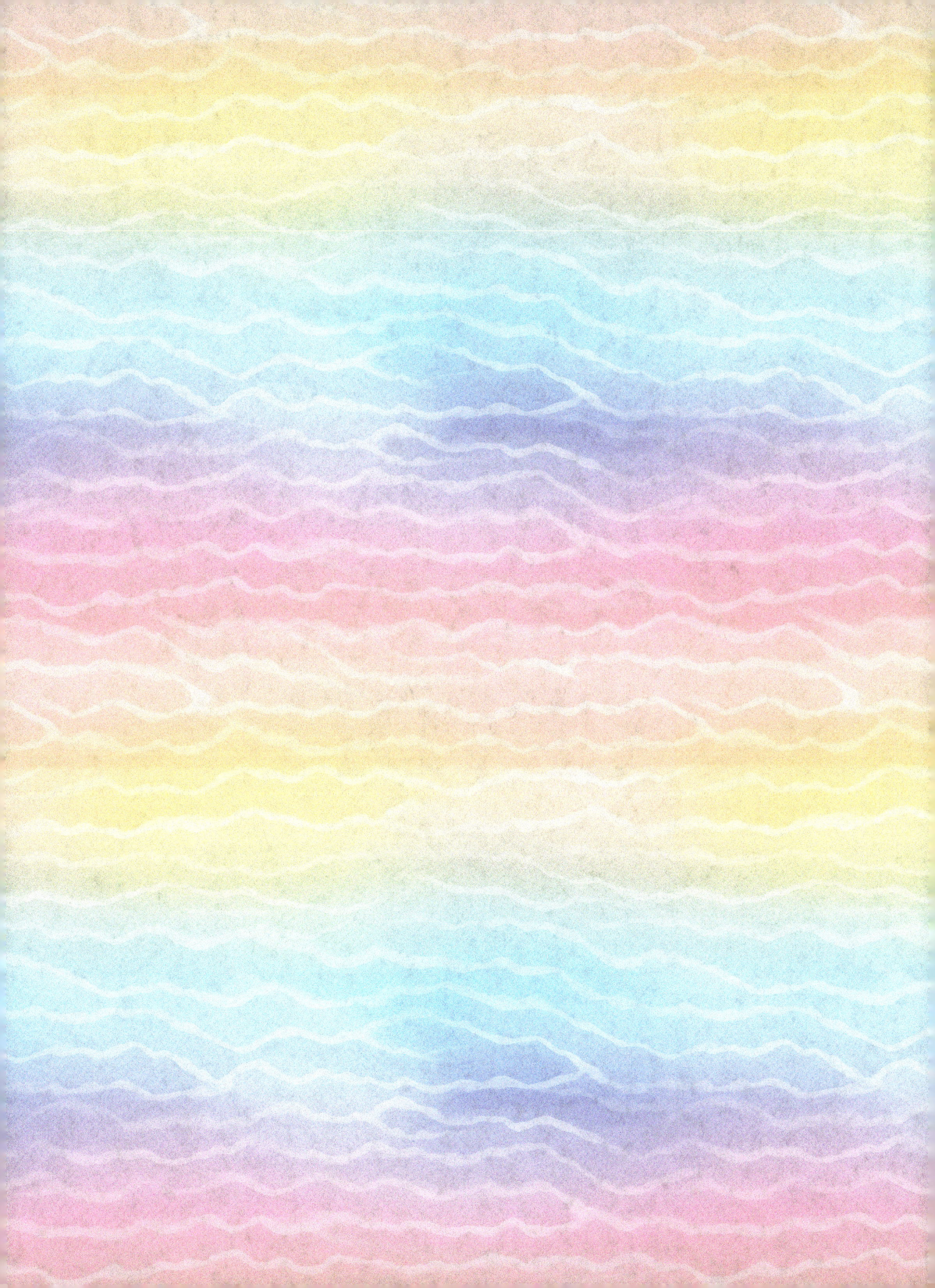

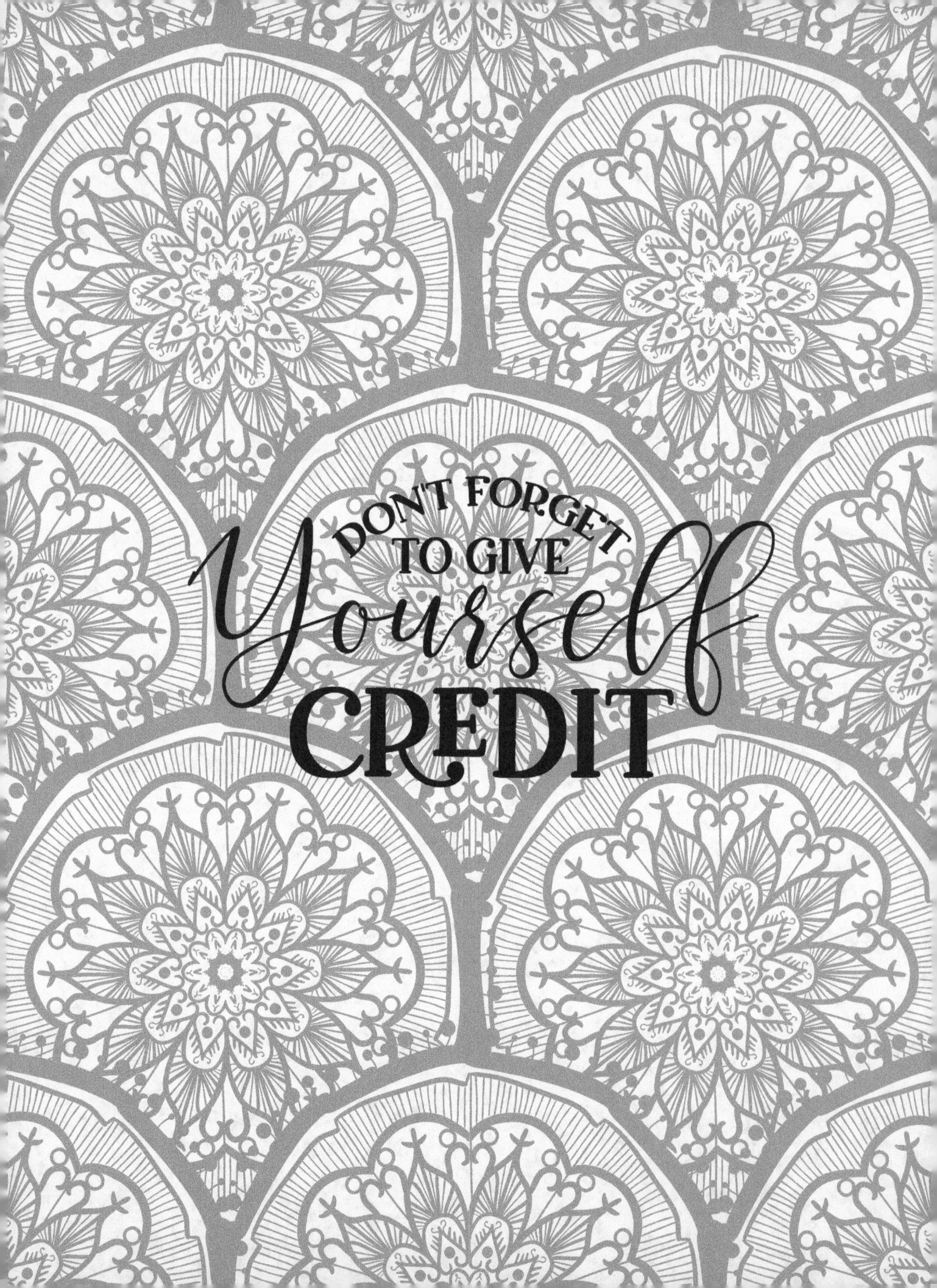

DON'T FORGET TO GIVE *Yourself* CREDIT

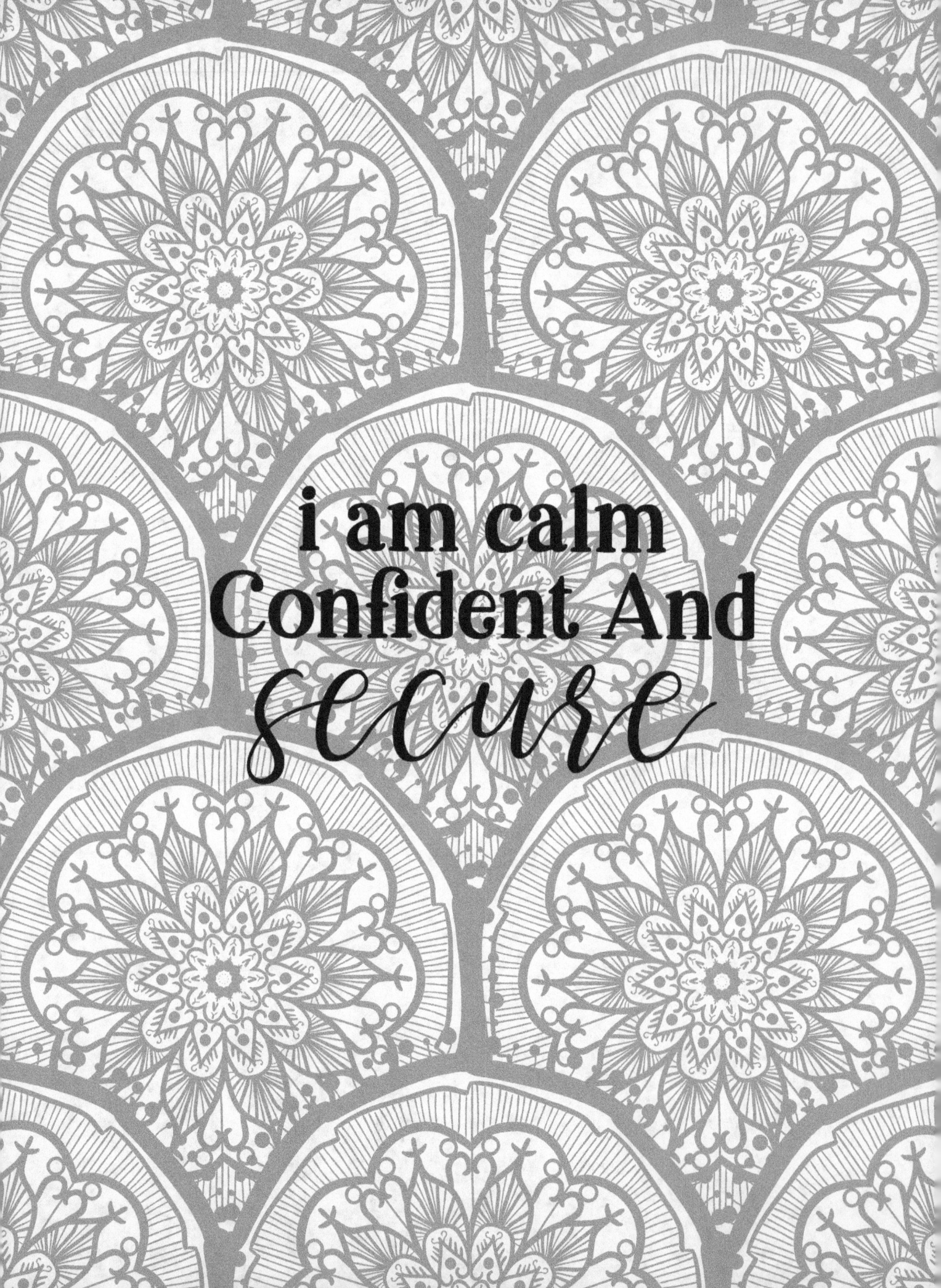

i am calm
Confident And
SECURE

i am
worthy
Wonderful
and wise

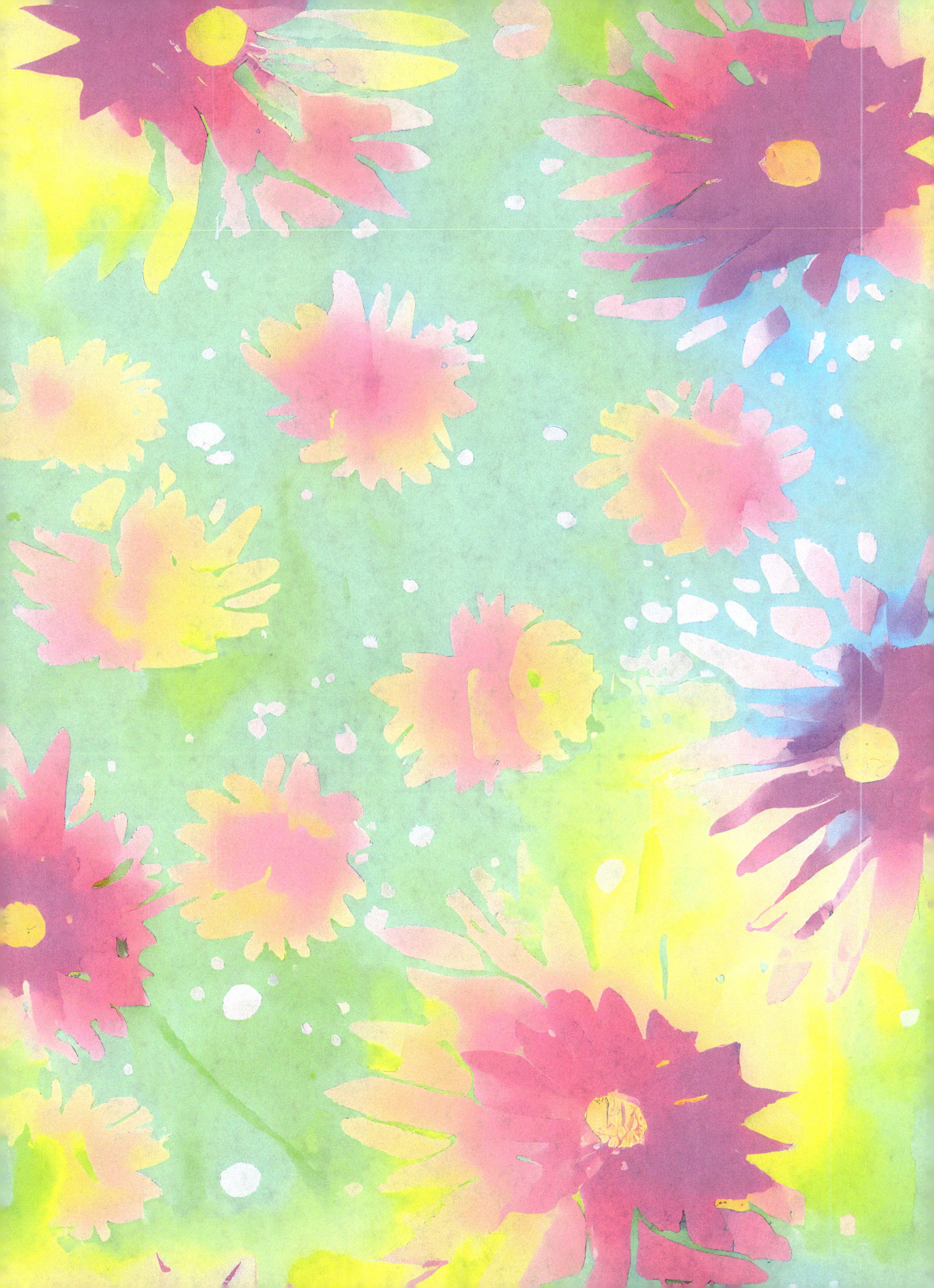

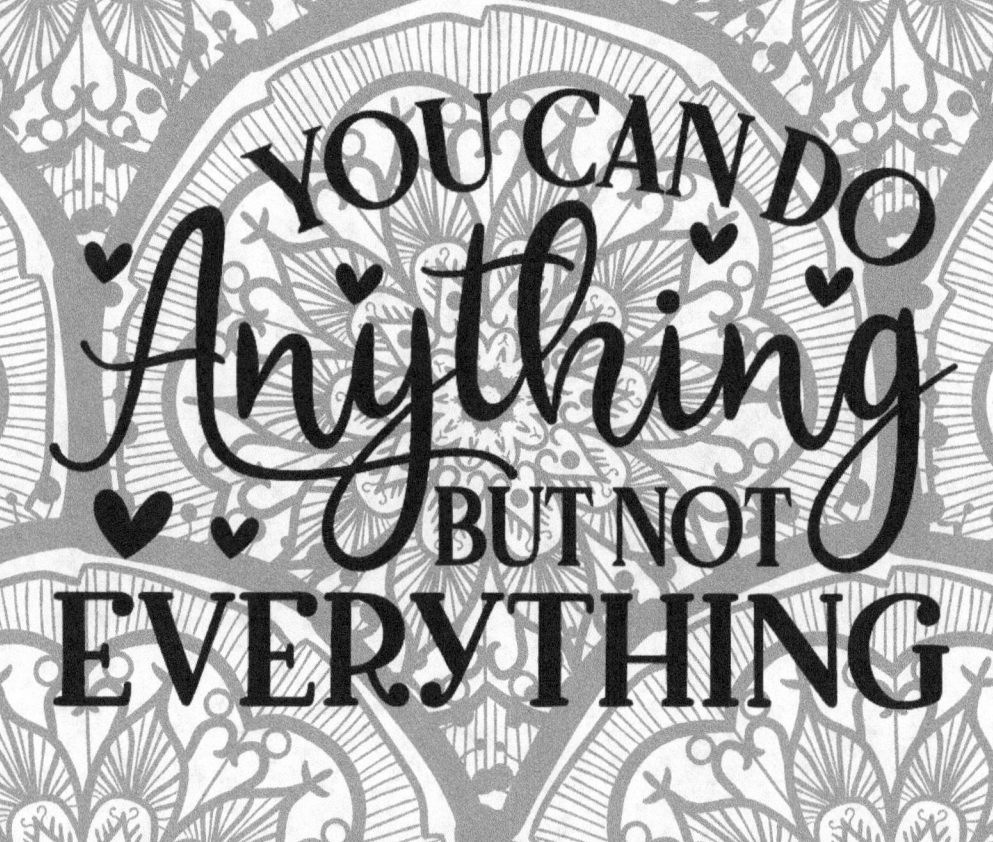

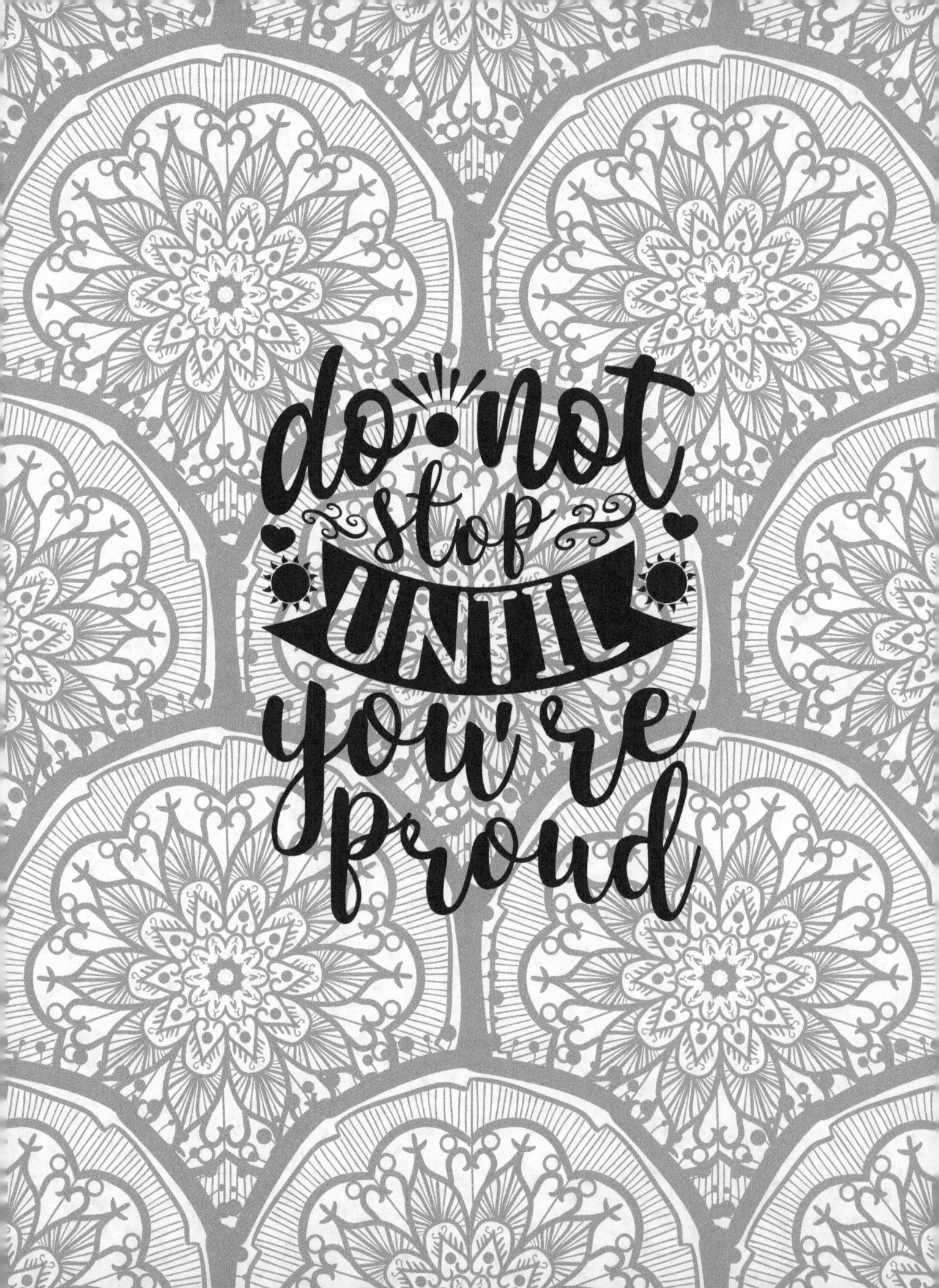

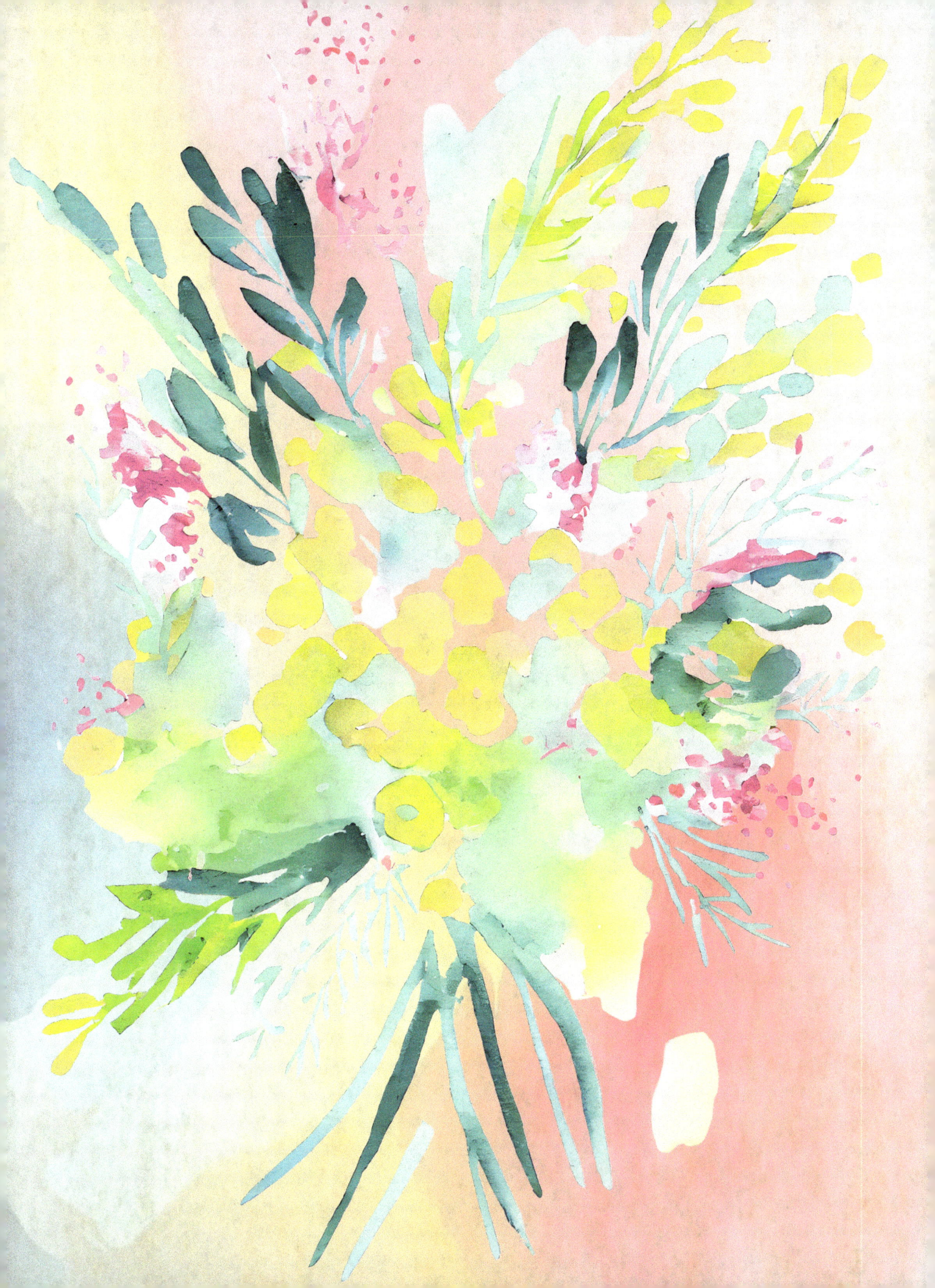

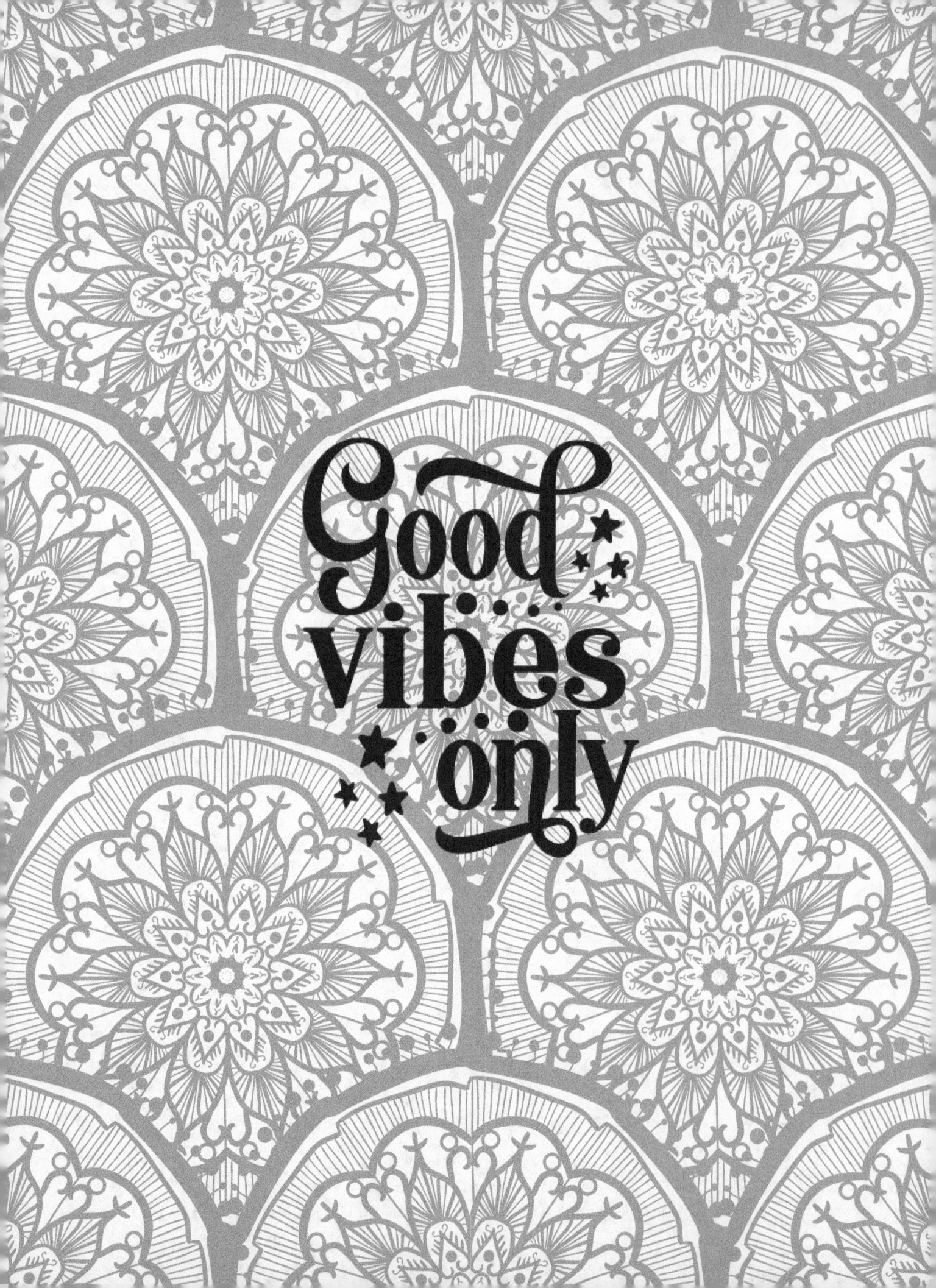

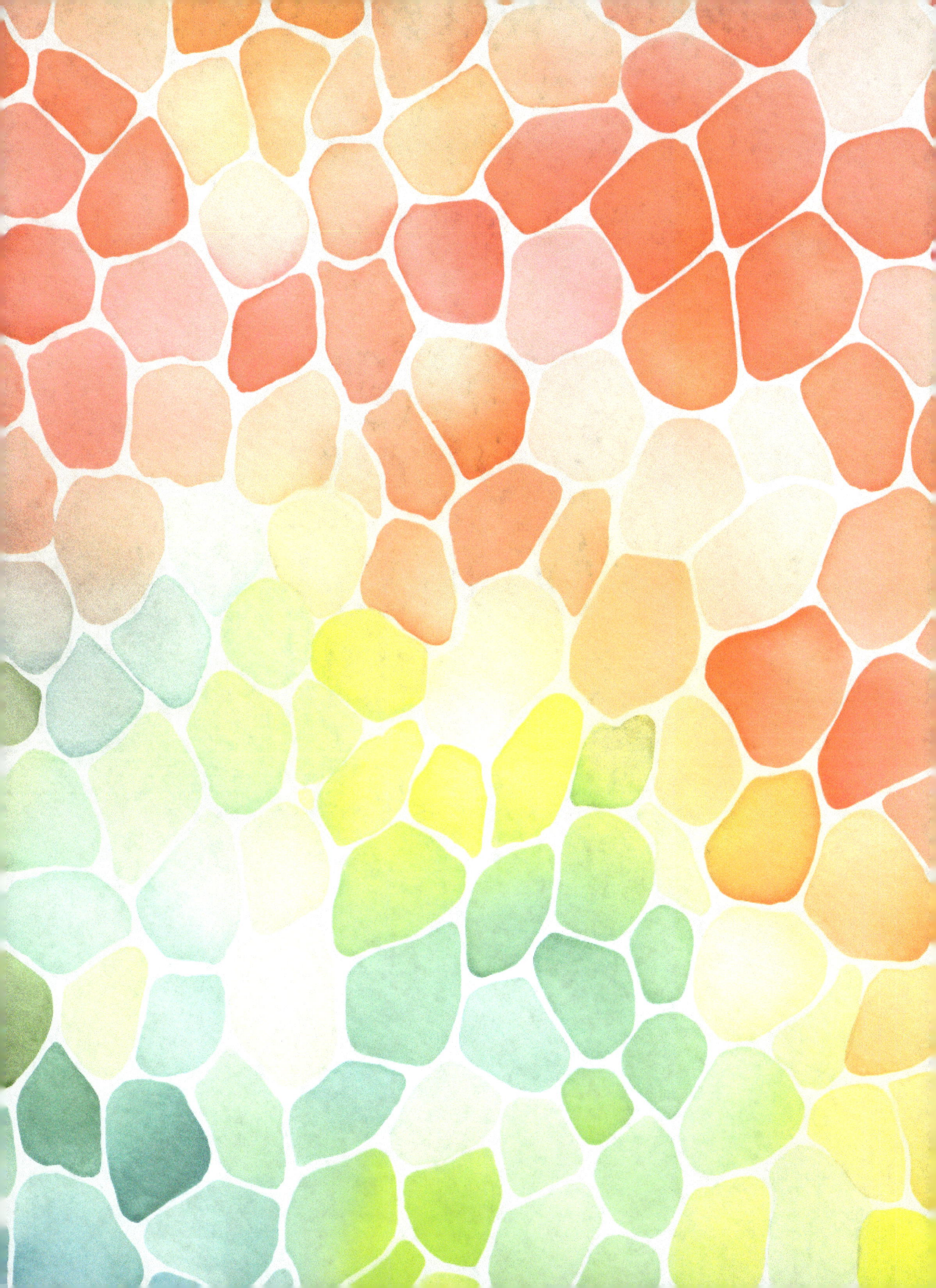

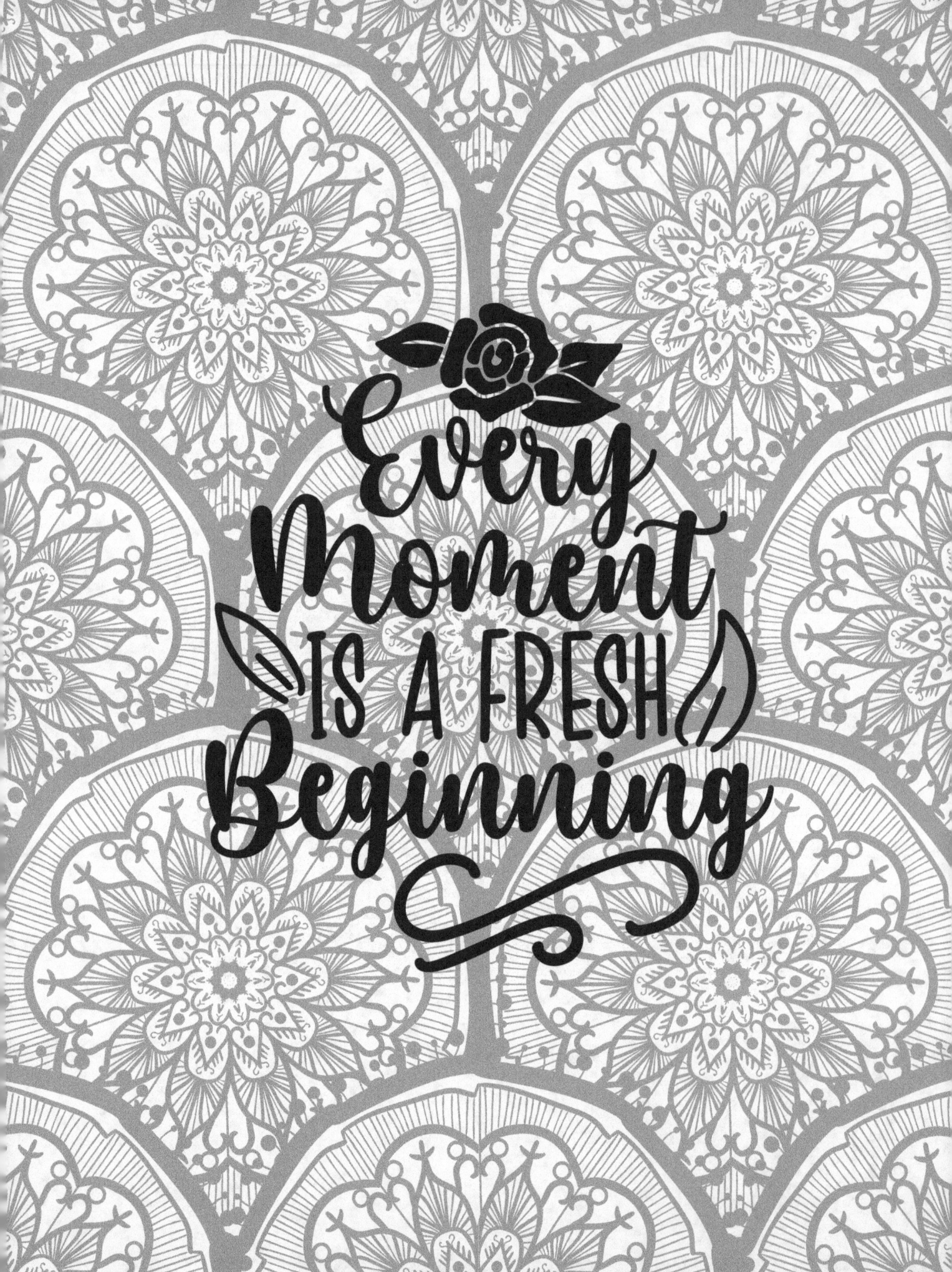

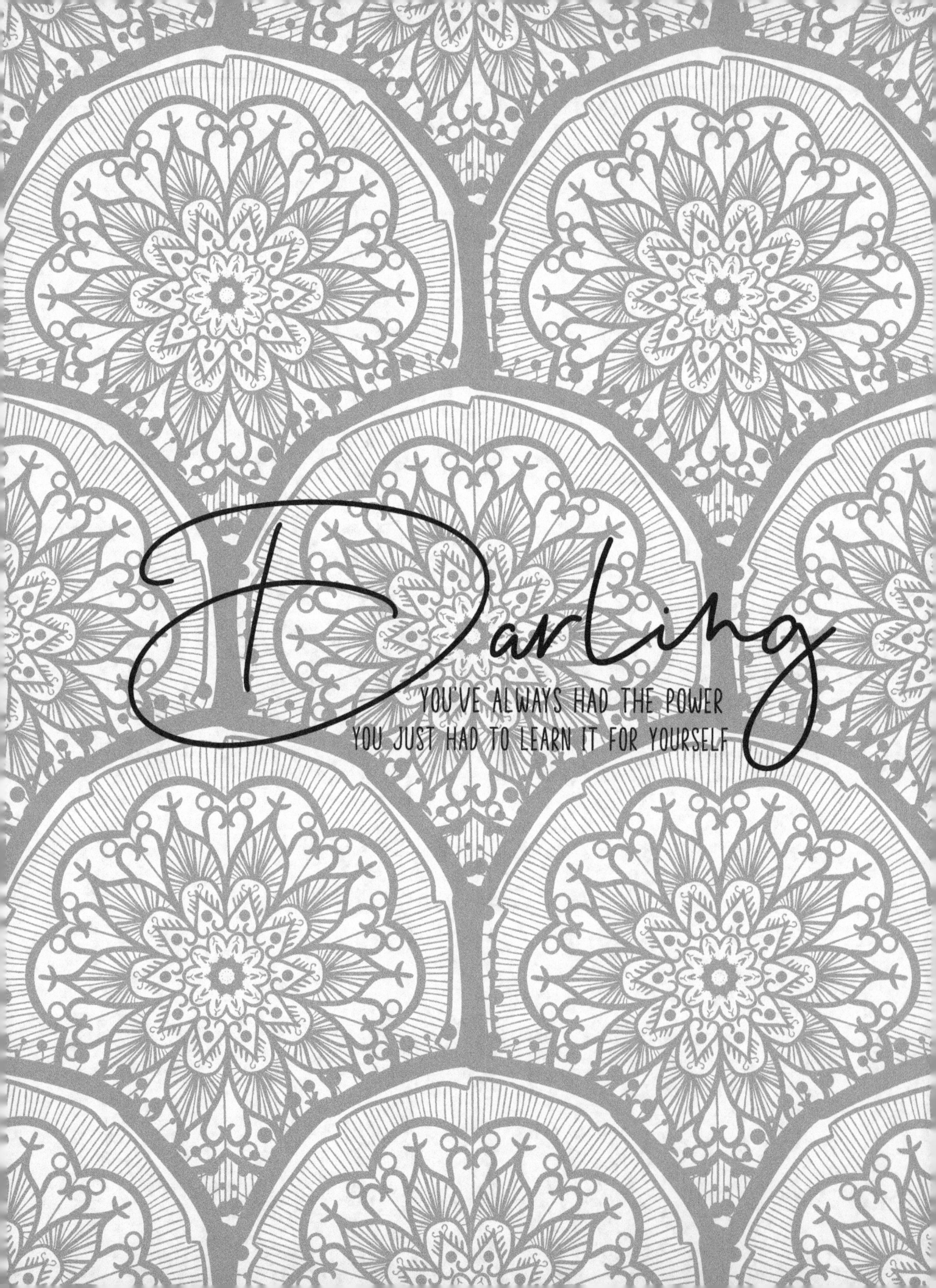

Darling
YOU'VE ALWAYS HAD THE POWER
YOU JUST HAD TO LEARN IT FOR YOURSELF

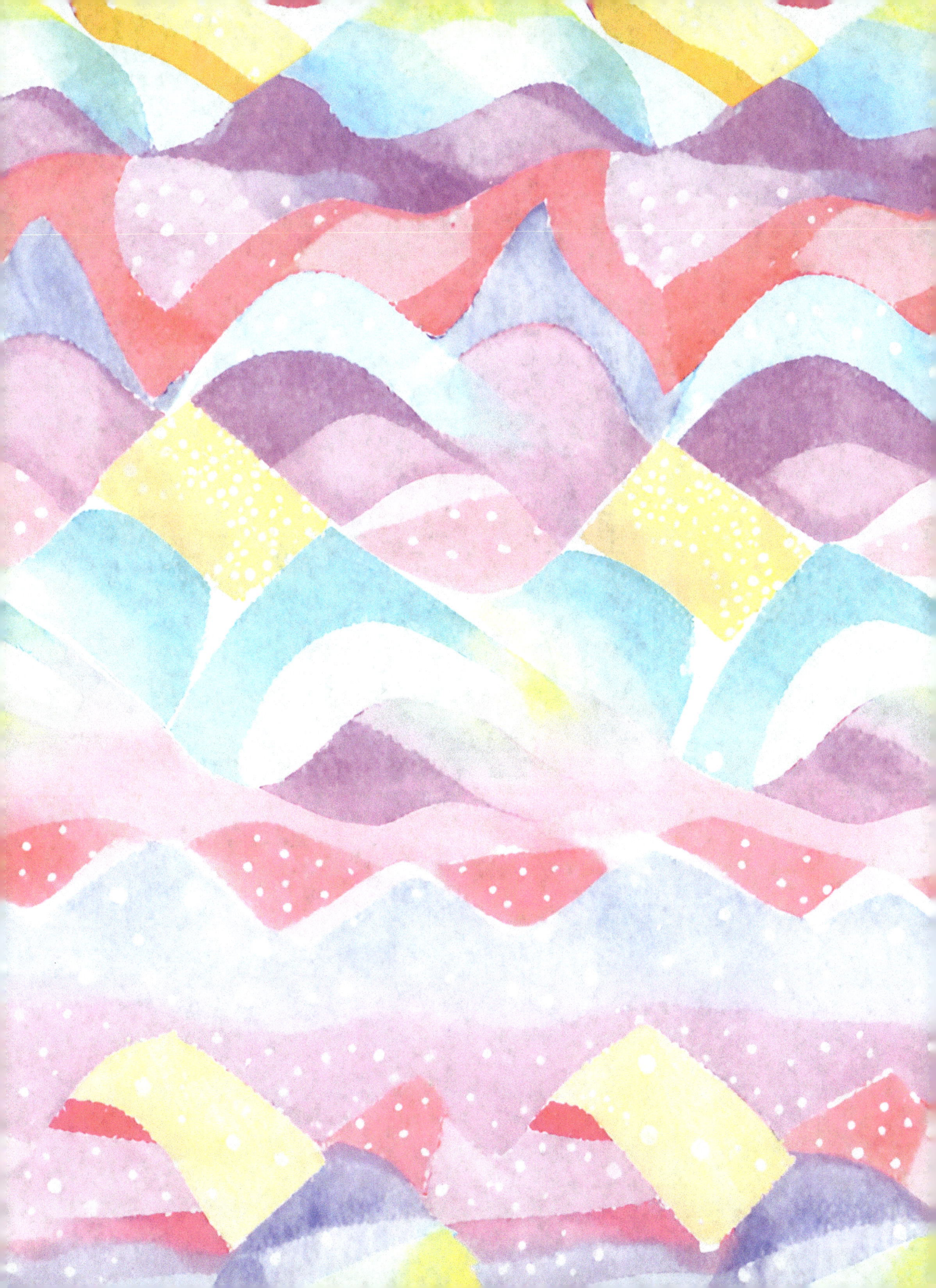

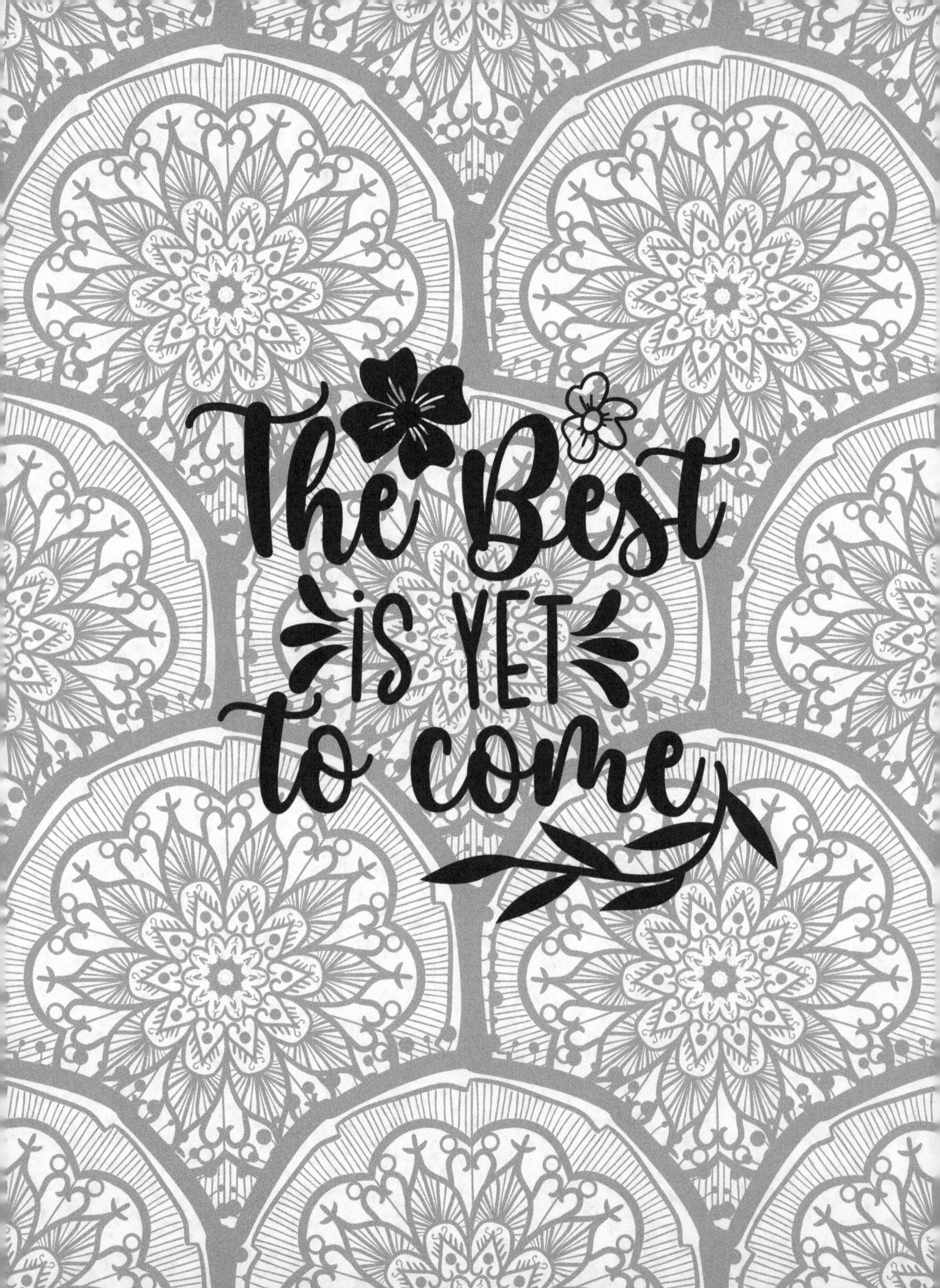

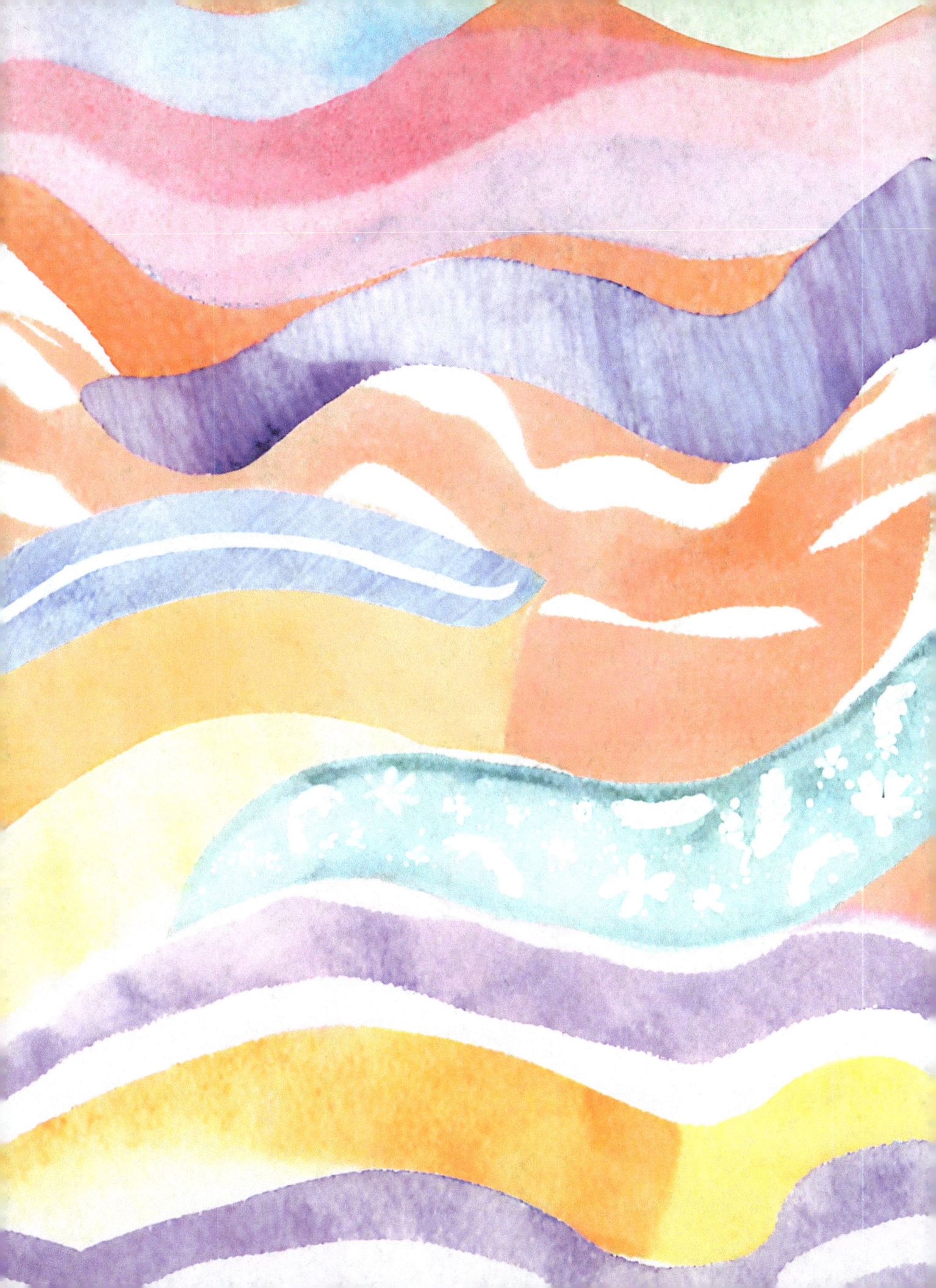

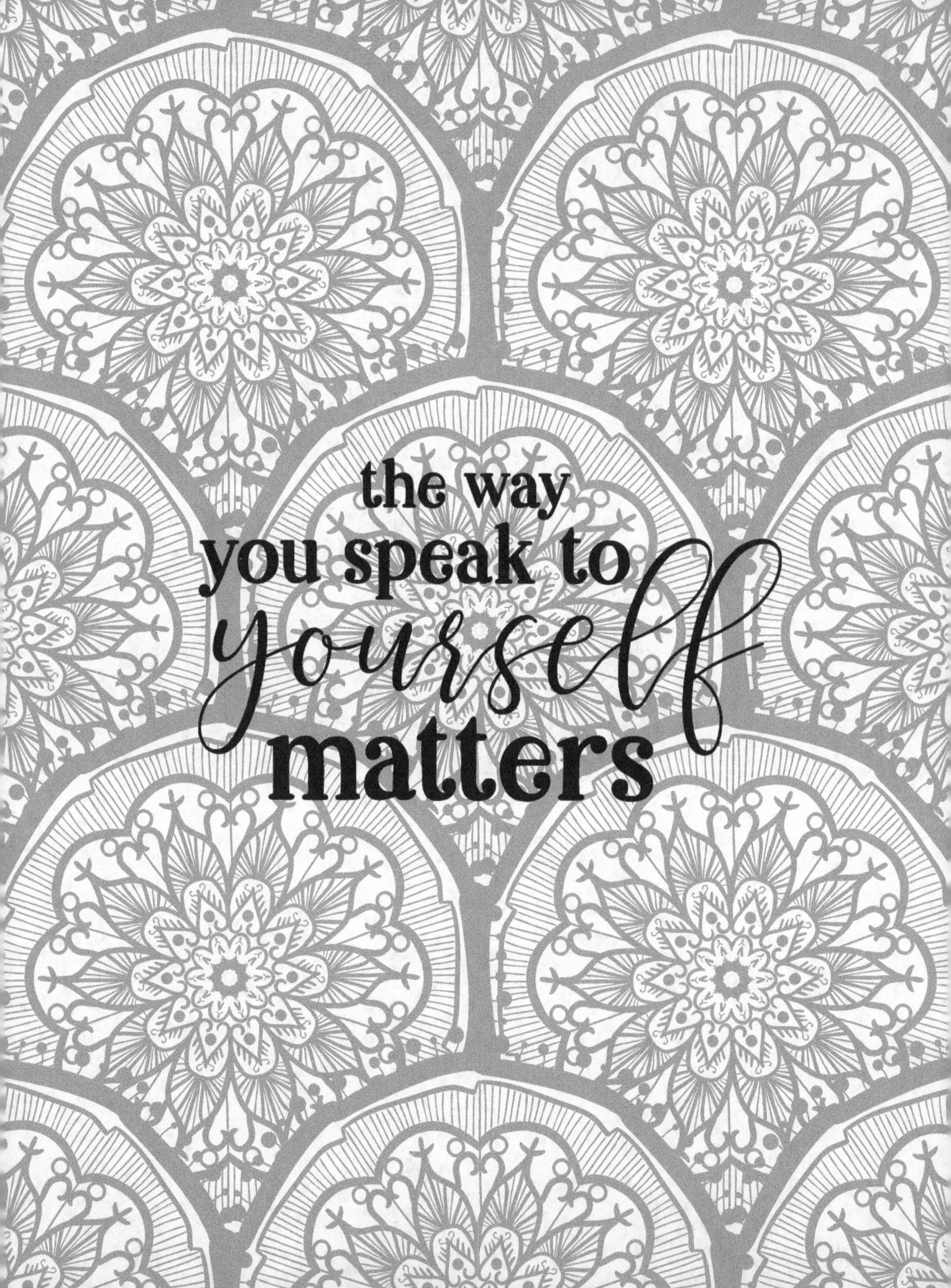

the way
you speak to
yourself
matters

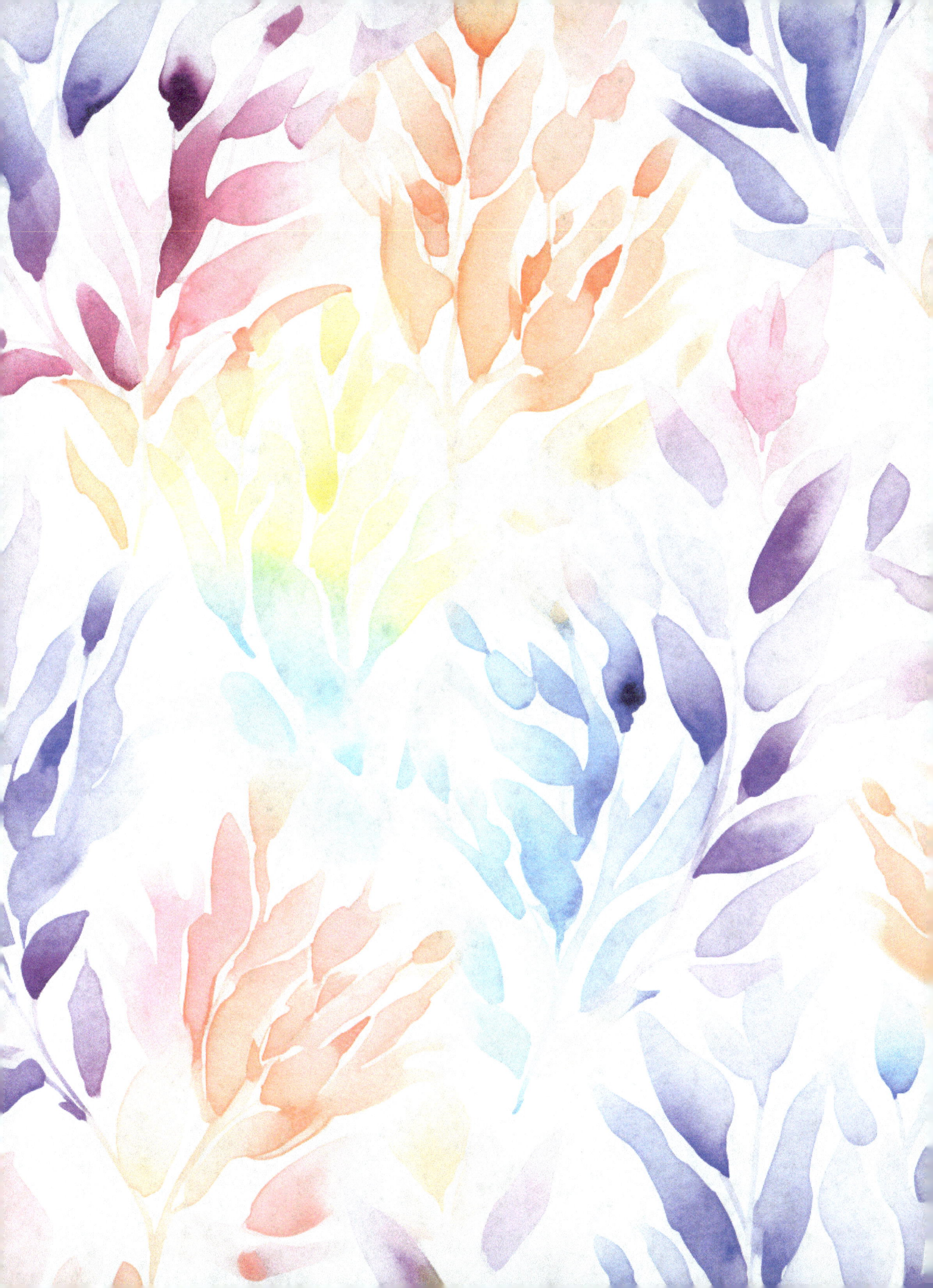

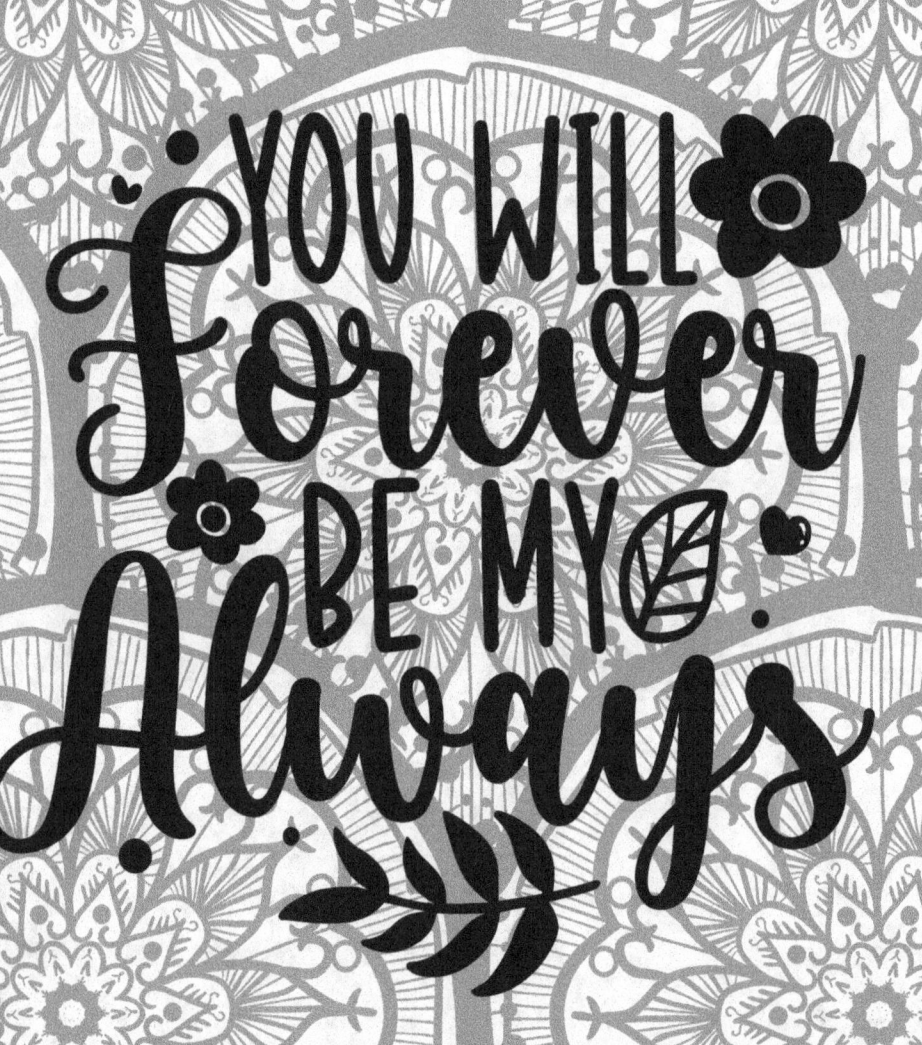

WISH LESS
Work more

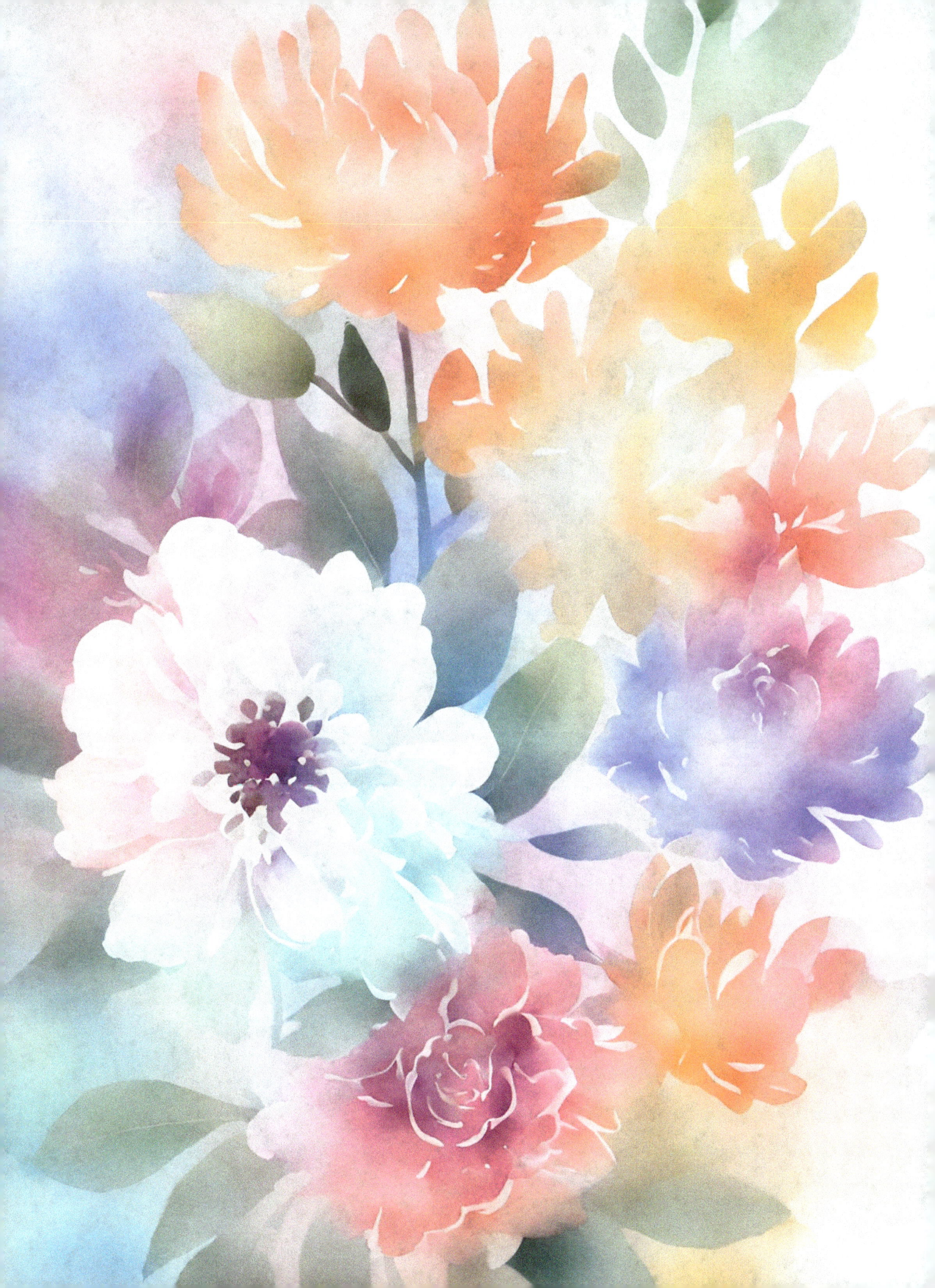

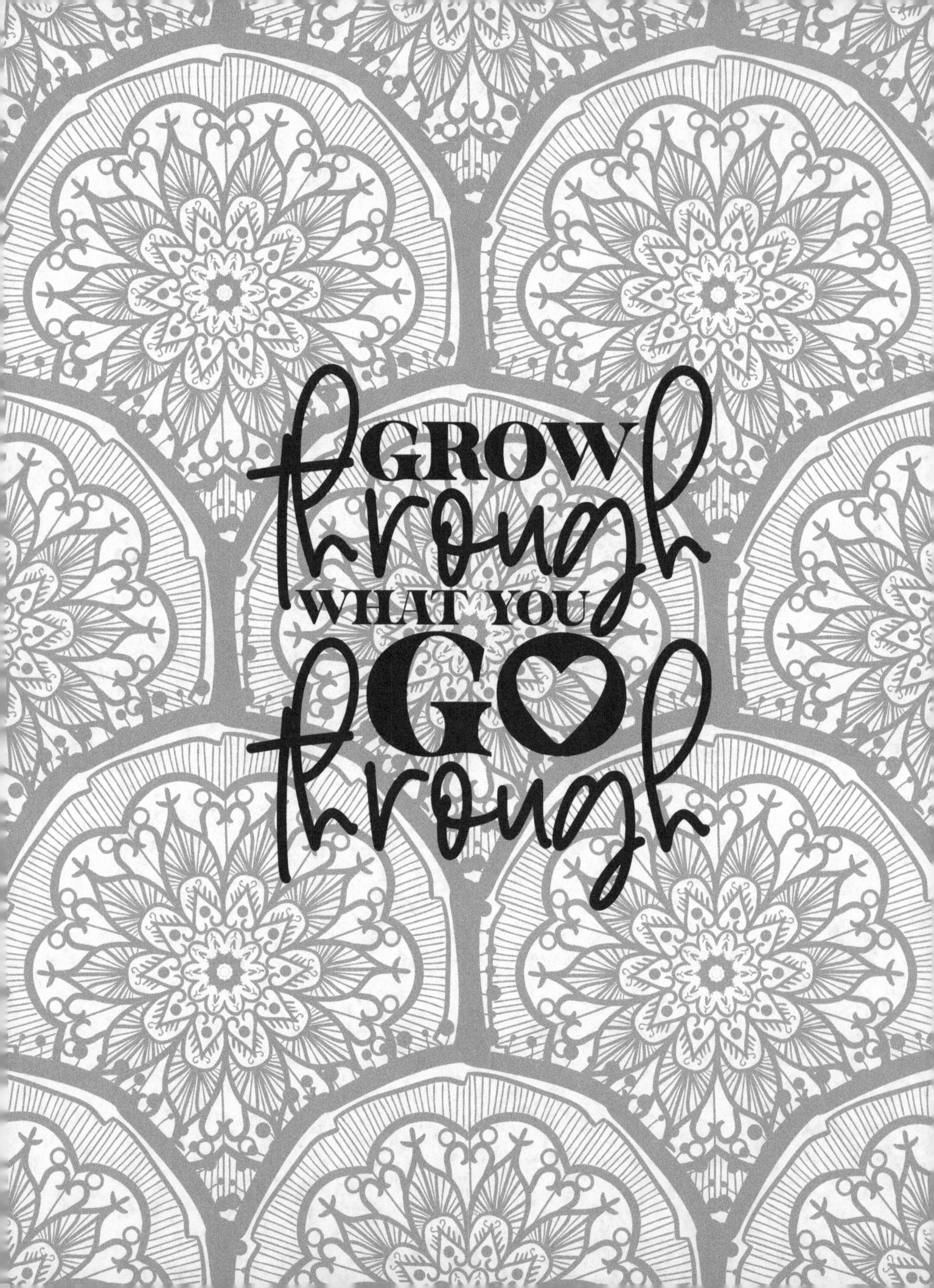

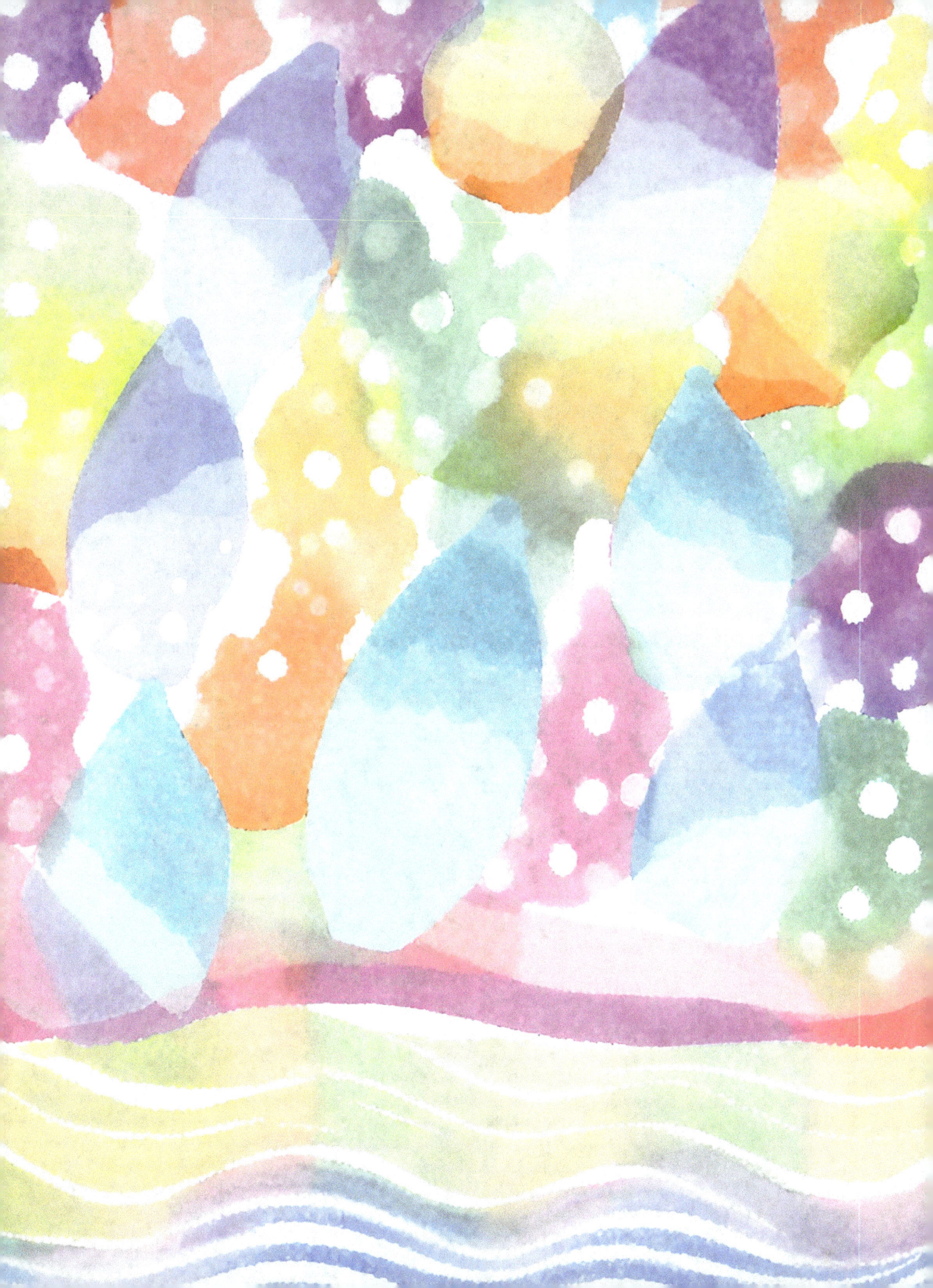

BECOME A

Priority

IN YOUR LIFE

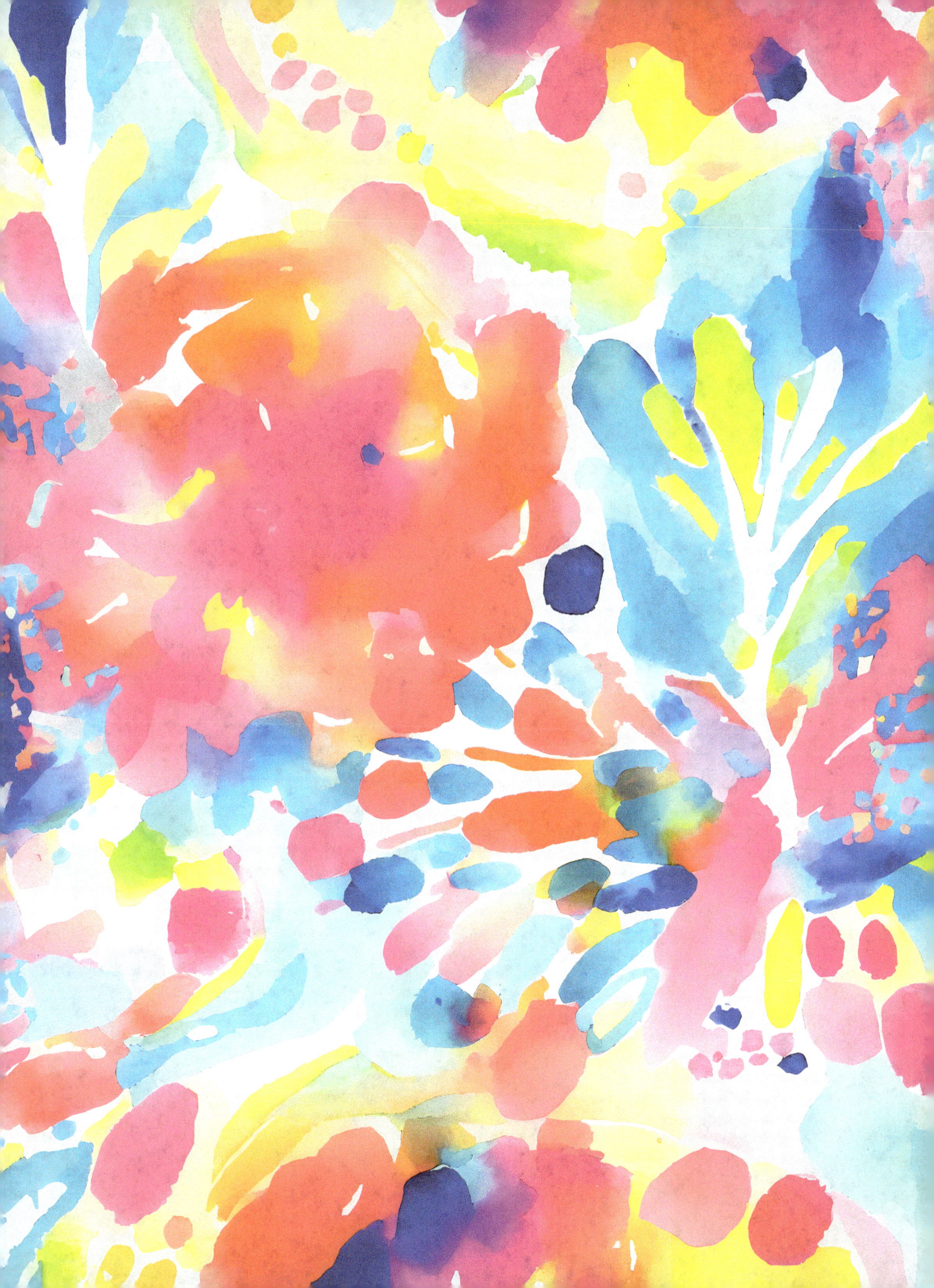

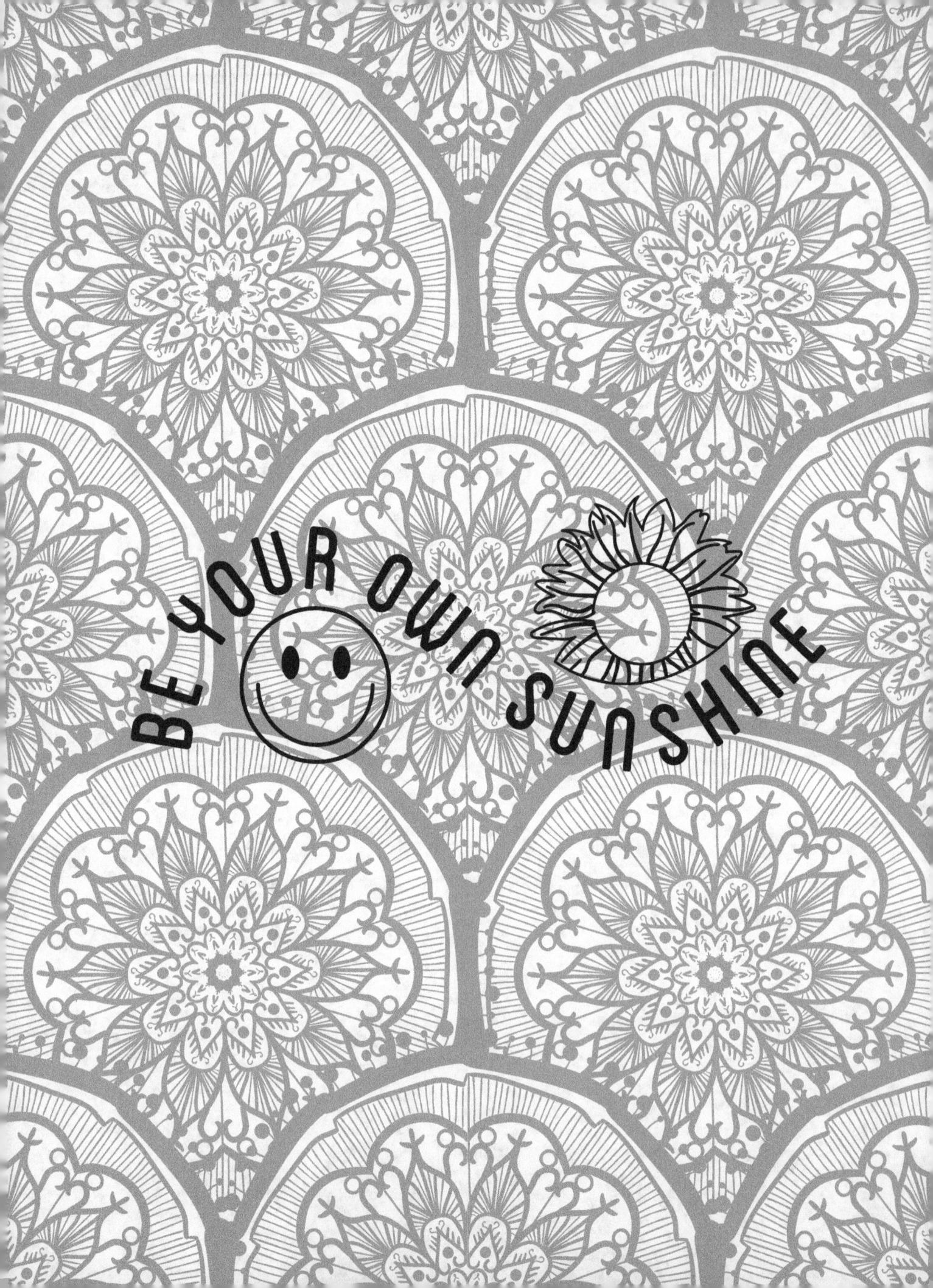

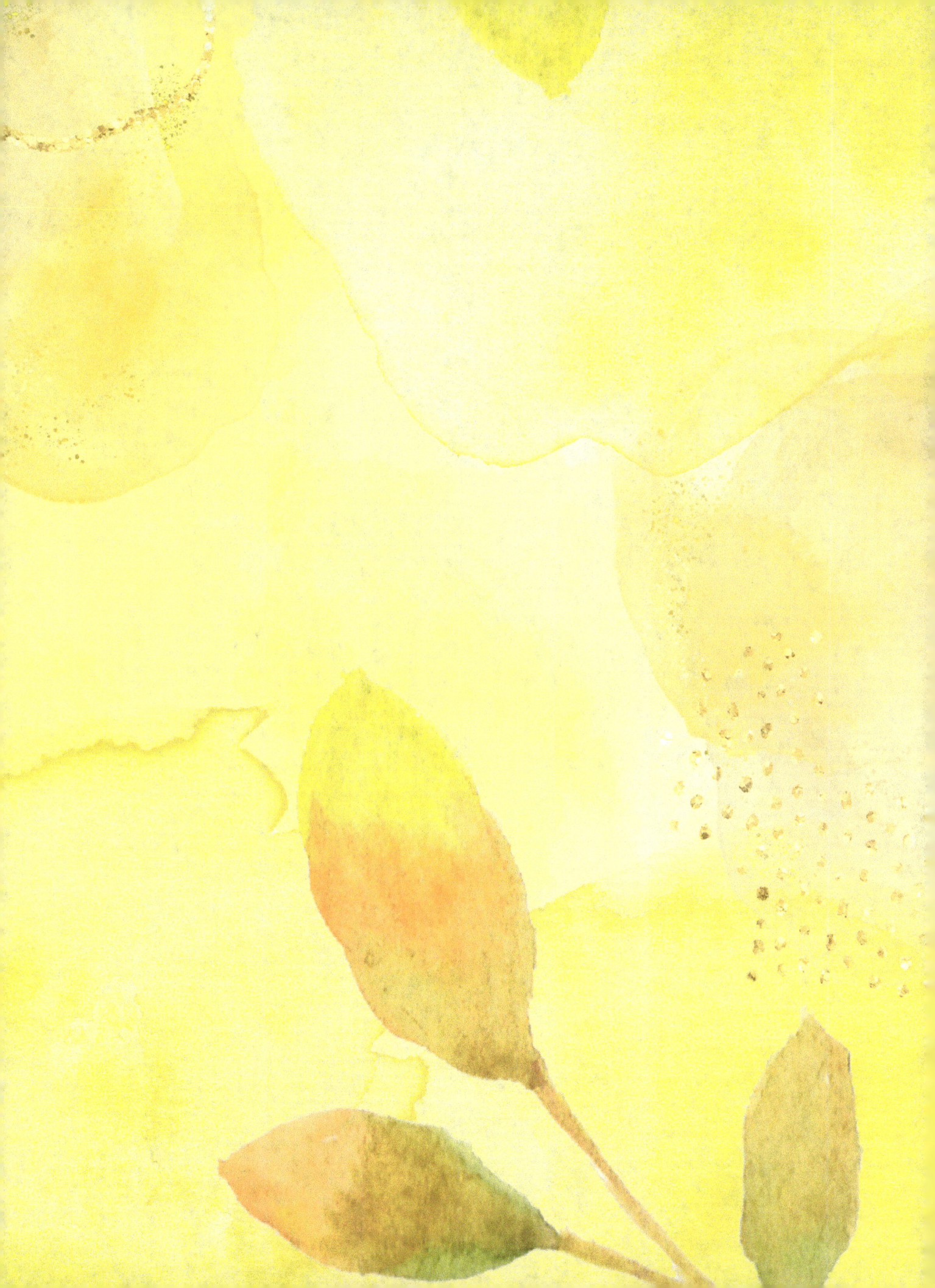

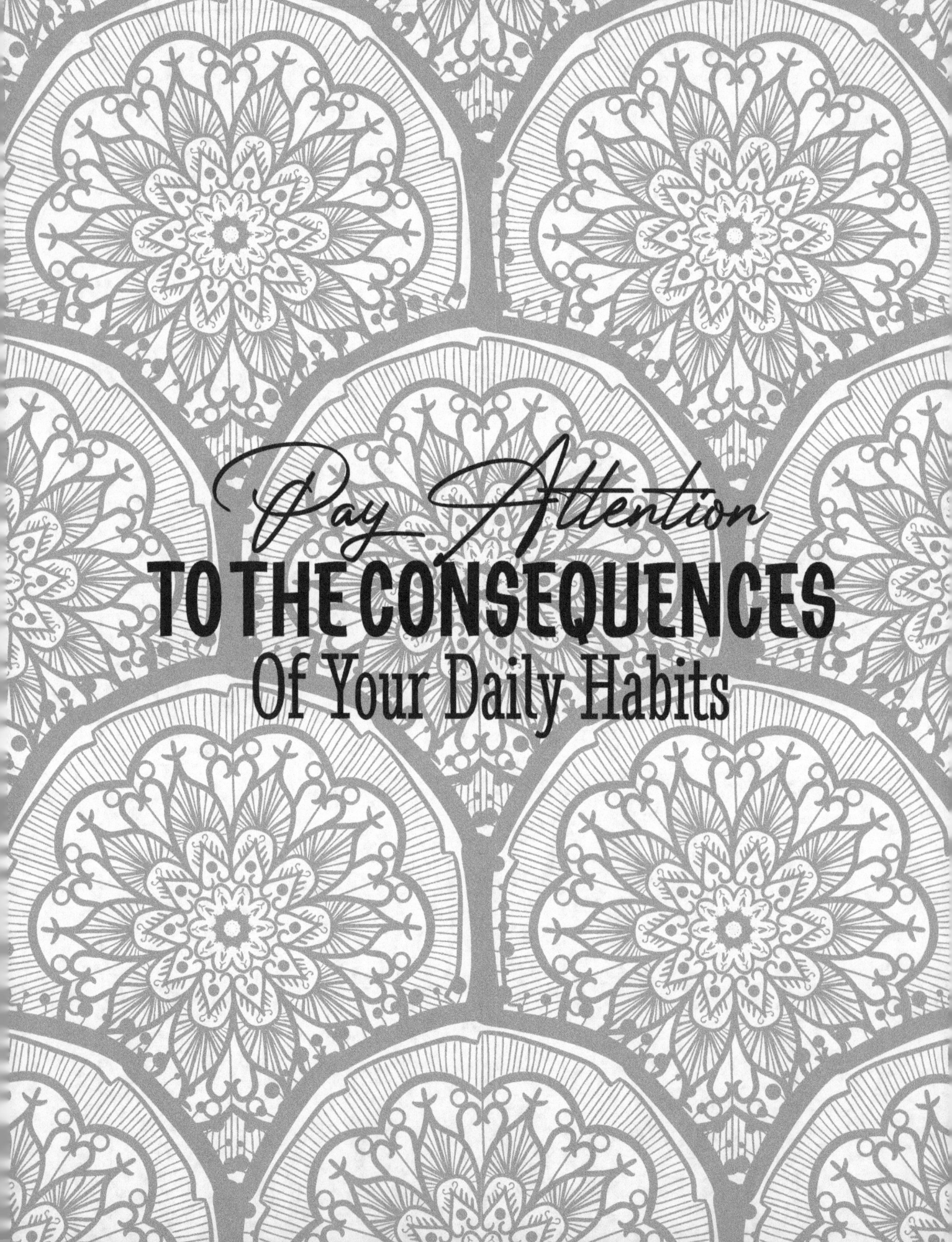

Pay Attention

TO THE CONSEQUENCES
Of Your Daily Habits

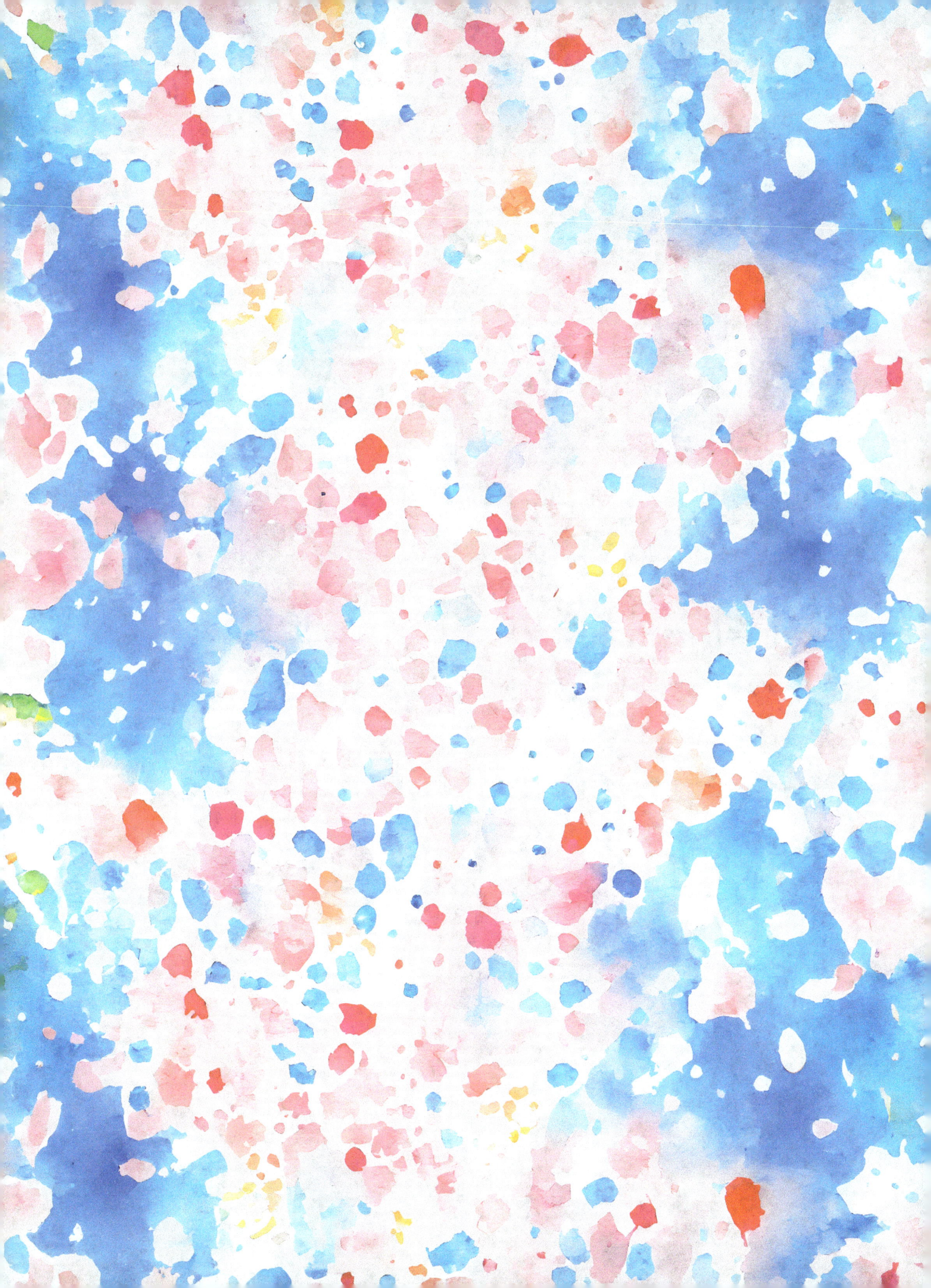

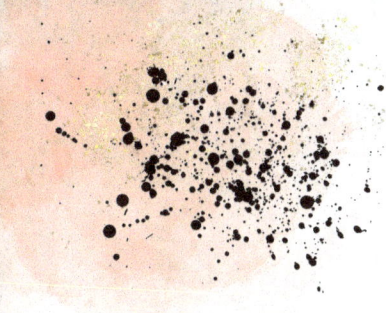

Did you enjoy this adventure?

Please visit our website to learn about the latest news we have for you:

www.auraeditions.com

But that's not all. We also have A SPECIAL GIFT FOR YOU! Just visit:

https://ko-fi.com/s/5a6dbce010

Your redemption code is AMZN-RCBFE01
Don't wait! Redeem your code now because it's only available for a limited time.

Your feedback is invaluable to us, so please do not hesitate to contact us, if you had the opportunity to provide a review, we would greatly appreciate it!

Don't forget to follow us on Instagram and TikTok: aura.editions

Thank you for your support!

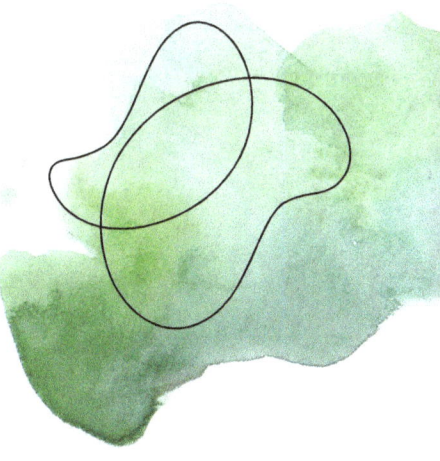

www.ingramcontent.com/pod-product-compliance
Lightning Source LLC
Chambersburg PA
CBHW082139290526
45794CB00008B/3097